2003

Animal Experimentation

OPPOSING VIEWPOINTS®

Animal Experimentation

OPPOSING VIEWPOINTS®

Other Books of Related Interest

Animal Experimentation

OPPOSING VIEWPOINTS ®

Helen Cothran, *Book Editor*

Daniel Leone, *President*

Bonnie Szumski, *Publisher*

Scott Barbour, *Managing Editor*

OPPOSING VIEWPOINTS® SERIES

GREENHAVEN PRESS
SAN DIEGO, CALIFORNIA

GALE GROUP

™

THOMSON LEARNING

Detroit • New York • San Diego • San Francisco
Boston • New Haven, Conn. • Waterville, Maine
London • Munich

Cover photo: Digital Vision

Library of Congress Cataloging-in-Publication Data

Animal experimentation : opposing viewpoints / Helen Cothran,
    book editor.
        p. cm. — (Opposing viewpoints series)
        Includes bibliographical references and index.
        ISBN 0-7377-0902-2 (pbk. : alk. paper) —
    ISBN 0-7377-0903-0 (lib. bdg. : alk. paper)
        1. Animal experimentation. 2. Animal experimentation—
    Moral and ethical aspects. 3. Animal rights. I. Cothran, Helen.
    II. Opposing viewpoints series (Unnumbered)

HV4915 .A638 2002
179'.4—dc21   2001040790
                                                            CIP

"Congress shall make no law...abridging the freedom of speech, or of the press."

First Amendment to the U.S. Constitution

The basic foundation of our democracy is the First Amendment guarantee of freedom of expression. The Opposing Viewpoints Series is dedicated to the concept of this basic freedom and the idea that it is more important to practice it than to enshrine it.

Contents

Why Consider Opposing Viewpoints?

"The only way in which a human being can make some approach to knowing the whole of a subject is by hearing what can be said about it by persons of every variety of opinion and studying all modes in which it can be looked at by every character of mind. No wise man ever acquired his wisdom in any mode but this."

John Stuart Mill

In our media-intensive culture it is not difficult to find differing opinions. Thousands of newspapers and magazines and dozens of radio and television talk shows resound with differing points of view. The difficulty lies in deciding which opinion to agree with and which "experts" seem the most credible. The more inundated we become with differing opinions and claims, the more essential it is to hone critical reading and thinking skills to evaluate these ideas. Opposing Viewpoints books address this problem directly by presenting stimulating debates that can be used to enhance and teach these skills. The varied opinions contained in each book examine many different aspects of a single issue. While examining these conveniently edited opposing views, readers can develop critical thinking skills such as the ability to compare and contrast authors' credibility, facts, argumentation styles, use of persuasive techniques, and other stylistic tools. In short, the Opposing Viewpoints Series is an ideal way to attain the higher-level thinking and reading skills so essential in a culture of diverse and contradictory opinions.

In addition to providing a tool for critical thinking, Opposing Viewpoints books challenge readers to question their own strongly held opinions and assumptions. Most people form their opinions on the basis of upbringing, peer pressure, and personal, cultural, or professional bias. By reading carefully balanced opposing views, readers must directly confront new ideas as well as the opinions of those with whom they disagree. This is not to simplistically argue that everyone who reads opposing views will—or should—change his or her opinion. Instead, the series enhances readers' understanding of their own views by encouraging confrontation with opposing ideas. Careful examination of others' views can lead to the readers' understanding of the logical inconsistencies in their own opinions, perspective on why they hold an opinion, and the consideration of the possibility that their opinion requires further evaluation.

Evaluating Other Opinions

To ensure that this type of examination occurs, Opposing Viewpoints books present all types of opinions. Prominent spokespeople on different sides of each issue as well as well-known professionals from many disciplines challenge the reader. An additional goal of the series is to provide a forum for other, less known, or even unpopular viewpoints. The opinion of an ordinary person who has had to make the decision to cut off life support from a terminally ill relative, for example, may be just as valuable and provide just as much insight as a medical ethicist's professional opinion. The editors have two additional purposes in including these less known views. One, the editors encourage readers to respect others' opinions—even when not enhanced by professional credibility. It is only by reading or listening to and objectively evaluating others' ideas that one can determine whether they are worthy of consideration. Two, the inclusion of such viewpoints encourages the important critical thinking skill of objectively evaluating an author's credentials and bias. This evaluation will illuminate an author's reasons for taking a particular stance on an issue and will aid in readers' evaluation of the author's ideas.

It is our hope that these books will give readers a deeper understanding of the issues debated and an appreciation of the complexity of even seemingly simple issues when good and honest people disagree. This awareness is particularly important in a democratic society such as ours in which people enter into public debate to determine the common good. Those with whom one disagrees should not be regarded as enemies but rather as people whose views deserve careful examination and may shed light on one's own.

Thomas Jefferson once said that "difference of opinion leads to inquiry, and inquiry to truth." Jefferson, a broadly educated man, argued that "if a nation expects to be ignorant and free . . . it expects what never was and never will be." As individuals and as a nation, it is imperative that we consider the opinions of others and examine them with skill and discernment. The Opposing Viewpoints Series is intended to help readers achieve this goal.

David L. Bender and Bruno Leone,
Founders

Greenhaven Press anthologies primarily consist of previously published material taken from a variety of sources, including periodicals, books, scholarly journals, newspapers, government documents, and position papers from private and public organizations. These original sources are often edited for length and to ensure their accessibility for a young adult audience. The anthology editors also change the original titles of these works in order to clearly present the main thesis of each viewpoint and to explicitly indicate the opinion presented in the viewpoint. These alterations are made in consideration of both the reading and comprehension levels of a young adult audience. Every effort is made to ensure that Greenhaven Press accurately reflects the original intent of the authors included in this anthology.

Introduction

*"Experiments are performed on animals that inflict severe
pain without the remotest prospect of significant benefits
for humans or any other animals."*

—*Peter Singer*

*"Virtually every medical innovation of the last
century—and especially the last four decades—has been
based to a significant extent upon the results of animal
experimentation."*

—*William Raub*

Public support for animal experimentation has declined
steadily over the past fifty years. In 1949, 85 percent of the
people in the United States were in favor of vivisection. By
1985, only 63 percent supported animal testing, by 1988
only 53 percent, and finally, in 1990, less than 50 percent of
those polled were in favor of it. Although these statistics indicate a steady downward trend in approval ratings over the
last half-century, an examination of the history of animal experimentation shows that such trends have traditionally
been transient. In fact, views on vivisection have fluctuated
wildly over the years.

Throughout history, scientists have alternated between using human and animal models for medical research. As early
as 370 B.C., the Greek physician Hippocrates used human cadavers to study disease processes. However, by the second
century, Roman physician Galen responded to growing religious admonitions against human autopsy by turning to the
practice of vivisection. Religious opposition against experimenting on human cadavers remained entrenched until the
Renaissance, when Belgium physician Vesalius began once
again to use humans in research. Religious leaders condemned
Vesalius as a heretic, but when the emerging scientific community backed Vesalius, he was eventually exonerated. Vesalius's methods remained dominant until the mid-1800s, when
a French physiologist named Claude Bernard reinstated ani-

mal experimentation. Bernard convinced the scientific community that theories of human diseases must be validated using animal models. From Bernard's time until the present, animal experimentation has been the preferred method of studying human diseases.

Vivisection in the United States became entrenched during and after World War II. During the war, scientists used animals to study the effects of explosives and munitions. In the decade after, government research institutes began expanding their animal experimentation programs and universities began to secure large grants for projects involving animal testing. In 1951, legislation introduced by then-Senator Hubert Humphrey guaranteed that the trend in favor of vivisection would continue.

Humphrey's bill mandated that most drugs require prescriptions. Whereas before, patients could go directly to their local druggist to obtain medicines, now patients had to go through doctors. Companies that manufactured drugs began to encourage doctors to prescribe their brand of medications, and in order to make those medications available as quickly and safely as possible, the drug companies relied increasingly on animals to test them. In 1961, the U.S. government mandated that all new drugs had to be tested on animals before they could go to clinical trial.

Although the general public was highly supportive of the biomedical community's reliance on animal testing after the war, scientists and activists around the world became increasingly concerned about the welfare of the animals involved in such experiments and the validity of the research. In 1959, British scientists William Russell and Rex Burch developed the "3Rs" approach to animal experimentation. Russell and Burch emphasized the importance of *reducing* the number of animals used in experiments, *revising* current practices to decrease the suffering of animals, and *replacing* animals with alternatives—such as the use of human tissue cultures—whenever possible.

Another change in the way that animal experimentation was conducted also occurred as a result of pressure from concerned scientists and activists. In 1966, animal welfare advocates succeeded in getting the Animal Welfare Act (AWA) passed. The AWA governs the way that lab animals are treated and determines which animals will be covered by its protections. Institutional Animal Care and Use Committees are charged with upholding the act and have provided increased oversight over the animal testing industry.

As animal use in laboratories exploded and concern over animal welfare increased, public opinion about the merits of vivisection began to change. Perhaps one of the most important events in the shift of public opinion was the release in 1975 of the book, *Animal Liberation: A New Ethics for Our Treatment of Animals*, by Australian philosopher Peter Singer. Singer questioned whether the information gathered from animal experimentation justified the amount of suffering imposed on research animals. His message that much of animal research was inhumane and wasteful influenced large sections of the public, and public pressure against animal testing increased. To combat Singer's negative message, scientists and medical organizations began to publish articles cataloging the many medical discoveries attributed to animal experimentation and to publicize the need for its continuation.

Today, the controversy surrounding animal testing is as vocal as ever. Those who are in favor of animal experimentation believe that animal testing is crucial to battling human diseases. Proponents argue that because animals and humans are biologically similar, findings from experiments on animals can be extrapolated to humans. Supporters also contend that alternatives cannot replace the study of living organisms. Many animal testing advocates base their arguments for vivisection on the claim that God ordained that humans are more important than animals and are entitled to use animals for human benefit.

On the other side of the debate are those who oppose animal experimentation. They believe that animal testing is invalid, unnecessary, and cruel. Opponents of vivisection maintain that animals and humans are different at a cellular level, which means that results derived from animal testing cannot be applied to humans. Those opposed to vivisection argue that alternatives are much faster and more accurate than animal tests. Opponents of animal testing contend that since animals and humans are both capable of suffering, both should be guaranteed the same right to life.

Due to the efforts of animal rights activists, the use of animals in research dropped by 50 percent in the period from 1990 to 2000. Yet support for animal testing from scientists, doctors, and patients remains strong. Experts in both camps continue the debate over vivisection in *Animal Experimentation: Opposing Viewpoints* in the following chapters: Do Animals Have Rights? Is Animal Experimentation Justified? How Should Animal Experimentation Be Conducted? Should Scientists Pursue New Forms of Animal Testing? Underlying all of these questions is the fundamental issue of humanity's relationship to animals. As feats of genetic engineering such as cloning and other new forms of animal testing become increasingly popular, it is likely that views about the rightness of using animals in medical experiments will shift yet again.

CHAPTER 1

Do Animals Have Rights?

Chapter Preface

Throughout the United States beagle dogs are used in laboratories as research models in the study of human diseases. People concerned about the plight of such animals divide roughly into two camps: Animal welfare advocates who work to make sure that animals used in research are treated humanely and animal rights activists who want to stop animal experimentation entirely.

The animal welfare movement was responsible for passage of the Animal Welfare Act in 1966, which set down rules governing the treatment of laboratory animals. For example, the act requires that dogs used in research be housed in clean cages, given toys to play with, and provided with human contact. Welfare proponents accept the human exploitation of animals provided that the animals are treated as humanely as possible. In general, these activists believe that humans have greater moral worth than animals. Columnist Stephen Schwambach articulates the religious underpinnings of the animal welfare position: "The difference between us and animals is that human beings are created in God's image and animals are not. Furthermore, God placed us over the entire animal kingdom."

Conversely, animal rights proponents do not accept the human exploitation of animals in any form. Advocates of this philosophy contend that animals and humans have equal moral worth and are therefore entitled to the same rights. For example, animal rights activists do not want cleaner cages for beagles—they do not want beagles used at all for biomedical research. Chris DeRose, director of Last Chance for Animals, an animal rights organization, illustrates his uncompromising position against animal research by saying, "if the death of one rat cured all diseases, it wouldn't make any difference to me."

Most people would probably agree with animal welfare activists that animals should be treated as humanely as possible, but the debate about animal rights is controversial. At stake is a human-animal relationship that has benefited people for thousands of years. In the following chapter, activists on both sides of the issue argue whether animals have rights.

"It cannot be right . . . to treat other animals as if they were 'tools,' 'models' and the like."

Animals Have Rights

Tom Regan

Tom Regan is University Alumni Distinguished Professor at North Carolina State University and general editor of *The Heritage Project*, a fourteen-volume series on the foundations of philosophy. In the following viewpoint, Regan argues that non-human animals have the same rights as humans do because animals are similar rational and emotional beings. He contends that viewing animals as inferior constitutes speciesism, a prejudice similar to sexism and racism. Furthermore, Regan claims that treating animals equally fosters individual growth and helps society become more compassionate.

As you read, consider the following questions:
1. What did Charles Darwin say about the difference between animals and people, according to Regan?
2. What examples does the author provide to illustrate the injustice of violating the rights of the few for the benefit of the many?
3. According to Regan, what four things do all secular and religious traditions emphasize?

Excerpted from *The Philosophy of Animal Rights*, by Tom Regan (The Culture & Animals Foundation, 1997). Copyright © 1997 by The Culture & Animals Foundation. Reprinted with permission.

It is not rational to discriminate arbitrarily. And discrimination against nonhuman animals is arbitrary. It is wrong to treat weaker human beings, especially those who are lacking in normal human intelligence, as "tools" or "renewable resources" or "models" or "commodities." It cannot be right, therefore, to treat other animals as if they were "tools," "models" and the like, if their psychology is as rich as (or richer than) these humans. To think otherwise is irrational.

The Philosophy of Animal Rights Is Scientific

The philosophy of animal rights is respectful of our best science in general and evolutionary biology in particular. The latter teaches that, in Charles Darwin's words, humans differ from many other animals "in degree, not in kind." Questions of line drawing to one side, it is obvious that the animals used in laboratories, raised for food, and hunted for pleasure or trapped for profit, for example, are our psychological kin. This is not fantasy, this is fact, proven by our best science.

The Philosophy of Animal Rights Is Unprejudiced

Racists are people who think that the members of their race are superior to the members of other races simply because the former belong to their (the "superior") race. Sexists believe that the members of their sex are superior to the members of the opposite sex simply because the former belong to their (the "superior") sex. Both racism and sexism are paradigms of unsupportable bigotry. There is no "superior" or "inferior" sex or race. Racial and sexual differences are biological, not moral, differences.

The same is true of speciesism—the view that members of the species *Homo sapiens* are superior to members of every other species simply because human beings belong to one's own (the "superior") species. For there is no "superior" species. To think otherwise is to be no less prejudiced than racists or sexists.

The Philosophy of Animal Rights Is Just

Justice is the highest principle of ethics. We are not to commit or permit injustice so that good may come, not to violate the rights of the few so that the many might benefit. Slavery

Can They Suffer?

The day *may* come when the rest of the animal creation may acquire those rights which never could have been witholden from them but by the hand of tyranny. The French have already discovered that the blackness of the skin is no reason why a human being should be abandoned without redress to the caprice of a tormentor. It may one day come to be recognized that the number of the legs, the villosity of the skin, or the termination of the *os sacrum*, are reasons equally insufficient for abandoning a sensitive being to the same fate. What else is it that should trace the insuperable line? Is it the faculty of reason, or perhaps the faculty of discourse? But a full-grown horse or dog is beyond comparison a more rational, as well as a more conversable animal, than an infant of a day, or a week, or even a month, old. But suppose they were otherwise, what would it avail? The question is not, Can they reason? nor Can they *talk*? but, *Can they suffer?*

Jeremy Bentham, quoted in *Animal Rights and Human Obligations* by Tom Regan and Peter Singer, 1989.

allowed this. Child labor allowed this. Most examples of social injustice allow this. But not the philosophy of animal rights, whose highest principle is that of justice: No one has a right to benefit as a result of violating another's rights, whether that "other" is a human being or some other animal.

The Philosophy of Animal Rights Is Compassionate

A full human life demands feelings of empathy and sympathy—in a word, compassion—for the victims of injustice, whether the victims are humans or other animals. The philosophy of animal rights calls for, and its acceptance fosters the growth of, the virtue of compassion. This philosophy is, in Lincoln's words, "the way of a whole human being."

The Philosophy of Animal Rights Is Unselfish

The philosophy of animal rights demands a commitment to serve those who are weak and vulnerable—those who, whether they are humans or other animals, lack the ability to speak for or defend themselves, and who are in need of protection against human greed and callousness. This philosophy requires this commitment, not because it is in our self-interest to give it, but because it is right to do so. This philosophy therefore calls for, and its acceptance fosters the growth of, unselfish service.

The Philosophy of Animal Rights Is Individually Fulfilling

All the great traditions in ethics, both secular and religious, emphasize the importance of four things: knowledge, justice, compassion, and autonomy. The philosophy of animal rights is no exception. This philosophy teaches that our choices should be based on knowledge, should be expressive of compassion and justice, and should be freely made. It is not easy to achieve these virtues, or to control the human inclinations toward greed and indifference. But a whole human life is impossible without them. The philosophy of animal rights both calls for, and its acceptance fosters the growth of, individual self-fulfillment.

The Philosophy of Animal Rights Is Socially Progressive

The greatest impediment to the flourishing of human society is the exploitation of other animals at human hands. This is true in the case of unhealthy diets, of the habitual reliance on the "whole animal model" in science, and of the many other forms animal exploitation takes. And it is no less true of education and advertising, for example, which help deaden the human psyche to the demands of reason, impartiality, compassion, and justice. In all these ways (and more), nations remain profoundly backward because they fail to serve the true interests of their citizens.

The Philosophy of Animal Rights Is Environmentally Wise

The major cause of environmental degradation, including the greenhouse effect, water pollution, and the loss both of arable land and top soil, for example, can be traced to the exploitation of animals. This same pattern exists throughout the broad range of environmental problems, from acid rain and ocean dumping of toxic wastes, to air pollution and the destruction of natural habitat. In all these cases, to act to protect the affected animals (who are, after all, the first to suffer and die from these environmental ills), is to act to protect the earth.

The Philosophy of Animal Rights Is Peace-Loving

The fundamental demand of the philosophy of animal rights is to treat humans and other animals with respect. To do this requires that we not harm anyone just so that we ourselves or others might benefit. This philosophy therefore is totally opposed to military aggression. It is a philosophy of peace. But it is a philosophy that extends the demand for peace beyond the boundaries of our species. For there is a war being waged, every day, against countless millions of nonhuman animals. To stand truly for peace is to stand firmly against speciesism. It is wishful thinking to believe that there can be "peace in the world" if we fail to bring peace to our dealings with other animals.

> "If an eagle has a legal right to life, isn't he
> bound to respect the same rights granted to
> the field mouse?"

Animals Do Not Have Rights

Charles R. Pulver

Charles R. Pulver argues in the following viewpoint that animals do not have the same rights as people do because animals
are incapable of fulfilling the duties that accompany such
rights, such as respecting life. Moreover, Pulver maintains
that federal laws already protect animals. Most important, the
author contends that God granted humans a higher status
than animals and encourages people to use animals. Charles
R. Pulver writes for the *Wanderer*, a Catholic newspaper.

As you read, consider the following questions:
1. What duty would a grizzly bear have if given the right
   not to be killed by humans, according to Pulver?
2. In the author's opinion, why can't animals be held to a
   set of legal duties?
3. What federal laws does the author cite as evidence that
   animals are already protected?

It has always been a firmly held concept in the fields of law, ethics, and government that for every right we enjoy, there is a corresponding duty which we must fulfill. For example, if we enjoy freedom of speech, we must respect other folks' rights to the same freedom. We cannot attempt to stifle another's speech while asserting our own. Likewise, we cannot morally claim the right to life for ourselves but deny it to others. Rights and duties are two sides of the same coin; we cannot in conscience separate the two.

The Duties of Bears and Eagles

So—if animal rights proponents are to claim any sort of credibility at all, they should factor in the notion of animal *duties* as an *intrinsic link* to whatever "rights" they attribute to our furry and feathered friends. Let's say that grizzly bears have a legal right to live—and not be hunted or harmed by humans. The bear, for his part, would then have a duty to not kill or harm humans. And if he does come after a human with intent to do harm, his right to live is forfeit and he may be killed by his intended victim, who acts in self-defense. After all, if humans can kill each other in self-defense, why shouldn't animals (who fail in their *duty* to respect another's life) be subject to the same rule?

And what about animals' duties to respect each other's "rights"? If an eagle has a legal right to life, isn't he bound to respect the same rights granted to the field mouse? And if the mouse ends up as a tasty meal for the eagle, then shouldn't the eagle be punished for violating the mouse's rights? Of course, the eagle couldn't be punished unless first convicted of his crime of gobbling up the mouse.

This means, in turn, that the majestic bird must be read his Miranda rights [which must be read by police officers to those they arrest in order to notify them of their rights], be given counsel, and be tried by a jury of his peers. We may assume that his "peers" should be members of his own species, i.e., fellow eagles. Or perhaps mice should be included on the jury, since eagles would be strongly biased to favor the defendant. In the unlikely event of a conviction, what punishment would be imposed—and for what crime: premeditated murder, or something less, such as mouse-slaughter?

Would the convicted killer get life without parole or the death penalty?

So many questions. So few answers. But so it must be if animal rights are to have validity. Which, of course, they never can. The ridiculous scenario described above is just one way of illustrating the utter foolishness of so-called animal rights. . . .

Jeopardizing Human Dignity

Properly understood, the concept of a right—and the attendant ideas of duty, responsibility, law, and obedience—enshrines what is distinctive in the human condition. To spread the concept beyond our species is to jeopardize our dignity as moral beings, who live in judgment of one another and of themselves.

Roger Scruton, *City Journal*, Summer 2000.

We know that animals can never be held to a set of legal *duties*—like not killing each other—because they lack intellect and free will. Their behavior is governed solely by instinct; they cannot distinguish right from wrong; they have no moral sense as humans do. They cannot be punished for "crimes" against each other or against humans; they cannot even grasp such a concept—or any concept of any kind. They are programed by God to live and act solely according to their senses and emotions. The great Western writers have been affirming this repeatedly for the past 25 centuries. (Of course animal rights activists are trying to "deconstruct" Western tradition, which completely refutes their silly movement.)

Federal Protection

These misguided zealots are actually indulging in overkill, because animals—wild and tame—already enjoy many legal "rights" under the laws of the land. More precisely, humans are bound to obey strict *legal duties* in dealing with animals. At the state and local levels of government in the United States there are literally hundreds of laws which prevent cruelty to animals. Most of these laws carry stiff fines and/or jail time—and are strictly enforced. At the federal level we have the Endangered Species Act of 1973, a law that at first protected 109 species, but has since been expanded to cover nearly 1,200 varieties of animals and plants.

The enforcement of this federal statute has gladdened the hearts of animal rights fanatics for the past 25 years. Not only has it granted legal "rights" to the bald eagle and the grizzly bear, but also to their smaller cousins like the snail darter, the kangaroo rat, and the dung beetle. These tiny critters have blocked construction of power projects, rerouted the course of superhighways, and compelled people to choose between losing their homes and going to jail. This painful choice came to light in 1993 when California homeowners sought to disk [plow] their yards to create a firebreak against raging wildfires. The feds forbade them to disk because it would disturb the kangaroo rat—a violation of federal law— and bring fines and imprisonment. As a result, all undisked homes burned down; those who turned the soil saved their homes, but faced criminal penalties. . . .

Dominion over All Living Things

We must hope and pray that this foolishness will collapse upon itself, and that sanity will prevail against "animal rights." God's sentiments on this matter are found spelled out loud and clear in the first chapter of *Genesis*. In verse 26, God says: "Let us make man in our image . . . let him have dominion over the fish of the sea, the birds of the air, the cattle, and all the wild animals—and all the creatures that crawl on the ground." In verse 28, He commands Adam and Eve "to fill the earth and subdue it" and He gives them "dominion over" fish, birds, and "all the living things that live on the earth."

Apparently, Yahweh, Creator of Heaven and earth, and Lord of the universe, is not an animal rights activist.

"There is no doubt that animals experience a life. . . . Like us, animals can feel pain and fear, but also excitement and satisfaction."

Animals Are Equal to Humans

Animal Liberation

In the following viewpoint, the Animal Liberation organization maintains that since animals experience a life in the same way that people do, they deserve the same right to life, liberty, and security. The organization claims that since intelligence is not used to determine whether humans are entitled to basic rights, the lower intelligence of animals should not be used to exclude them from rights. Therefore, the organization argues that it is immoral to experiment on animals to benefit people. Animal Liberation is an international organization that works to protect the rights of animals.

As you read, consider the following questions:

1. What examples does the organization cite to illustrate that human rights have not always been respected?
2. What evidence does the organization provide to show that animals experience a life just as people do?
3. What is speciesism, according to the organization?

How do we know what is right? How should other people be treated? There are debates going on in society about many issues, so obviously there is no easy answer to these questions, even where humans are concerned.

Declaration of Human Rights

In the case of humans, the United Nations Declaration of Human Rights sets out a list of rights that people should have. These include:

- Everyone has the right to life, liberty and security of person.
- No one shall be held in slavery or servitude.
- No one shall be subjected to torture or to cruel, inhuman or degrading treatment or punishment.

According to the United Nations, a person may not be killed, exploited, cruelly treated, intimidated, or imprisoned for no good reason. Put another way, people should be able to live in peace, according to their own needs and preferences.

Who should have these rights? Do they apply to people of all races? Children? People who are brain damaged or senile? The Declaration makes it clear that basic rights apply to everyone. To make a slave of someone who is intellectually handicapped or of a different race is no more justifiable than to make a slave of anyone else.

The reason why these rights apply to everyone is simple: regardless of our differences, we all experience a life with its mosaic of thoughts and feelings. This applies equally to the princess and the hobo, the brain surgeon and the dunce. Our value as individuals arises from this capacity to experience life, not because of any intelligence or usefulness to others. Every person has an inherent value, and deserves to be treated with respect in order to make the most of their unique life experience.

Slavery and Genocide

The idea of human rights and inherent value has not always been accepted.

In previous centuries Africans were captured and taken as slaves to American plantations. They were cruelly treated, and many died or were killed. Families were split apart forever. Slaves were considered to be savages without souls. They were treated as objects to be exploited, with no regard for their feelings or their lives.

During the Second World War, Nazis not only killed millions of Jews in concentration camps, they also carried out scientific experiments on them. Jews were considered to be undesirable and not real humans deserving of respect.

In each case the perpetrators of these atrocities singled out groups that were in some way different, and claimed that they were inferior. This inferiority supposedly justified the appalling treatment. Both slave traders and Nazis denied the inherent value of their victims, and instead treated them as objects to be exploited or destroyed at will.

Animals Experience a Life

What about animals? Do they have inherent value? Do they, like humans, deserve respect?

There is no doubt that animals experience a life, certainly the vertebrates (animals with backbones), and possibly others. Like us, animals can feel pain and fear, but also excitement and satisfaction. Close contact with animals shows that they look forward to some events, and can clearly get a lot of enjoyment from their lives, be it from basking in the sun, exercising, eating favourite food, or interacting with others, as in playing and mutual grooming.

Certainly animals don't have the same abilities as humans. They can't talk, write books or drive cars, but neither can some humans. Do we say that humans who lack these abilities have no value and no rights? Certainly not, because those people still experience a life which can be filled with positive or negative events. We don't ask how intelligent a person is before we decide whether to eat them or experiment on them. Regardless of intelligence, their life still has value to them.

Exactly the same is true of animals. In spite of species differences, we have in common the capacity for experience. As philosopher Tom Regan has said in his argument for animal rights:

> . . . we are each of us the experiencing subject of a life, a conscious creature having an individual welfare that has importance to us

whatever our usefulness to others. We want and prefer things, believe and feel things, recall and expect things. And all these dimensions of our life, including our pleasure and pain, our enjoyment and suffering, our satisfaction and frustration, our continued existence or our untimely death—all make a difference to the quality of our life as lived, as experienced, by us as individuals. As the same is true of those animals that concern us (the ones that are eaten and trapped, for example), they too must be viewed as the experiencing subjects of a life, with inherent value of their own.

If the inherent value of humans means that they have the right to be treated with respect, then the same applies to animals. The points made earlier about human rights can be rephrased: animals may not be killed, exploited, cruelly treated, intimidated, or imprisoned for no good reason. Animals should be able to live in peace, according to their own needs and preferences.

Animal Rights and Experimentation

If each individual has inherent value, is it justifiable to harm one individual for the benefit of others? Is the evil of violating the rights of that individual outweighed by the good result that may come of it?

The Nazis experimented on Jews, and were condemned for it in the Nuremberg war crime trials. It is accepted that

---

The Similarities Between Species

Our thirty-nine years with wild chimpanzees at Gombe . . . has taught us much about these relatives of ours, each with his or her own unique personality. They share so many of our behaviors. They form close affectionate bonds with each other that may persist through a life of sixty or more years; they feel joy and sorrow and despair, mental as well as physical suffering; they show many of the intellectual skills that until recently we believed unique to ourselves; they look into mirrors and see themselves as individuals—they have consciousness of "self." Admittedly, chimpanzees are capable, as are we, of acts of brutality. But they also demonstrate empathy, compassion, altruism, and love. Should not beings of this sort have the same kind of legal rights as those we grant to human infants or the mentally disabled, who also cannot speak for themselves?

Jane Goodall, preface to *Rattling the Cage* by Steven M. Wise, 2000.

---

individual humans may not be forced to take part in harmful experiments, even though there is no doubt that better medical knowledge would be gained in this way than by experimenting on other species. This end (better medical knowledge) does not justify the wrong that is done to the individuals that are experimented on. The same principle applies to all people, including those that are brain damaged, senile or mentally ill. They have value in themselves, and are not objects to be used for the benefit of others.

The same is also true of animals. Using them as objects in experiments ignores their right to be treated with respect. To quote Tom Regan again:

> Lab animals are not our tasters; we are not their kings. Because these animals are treated routinely, systematically as if their value were reducible to their usefulness to others, they are routinely, systematically treated with a lack of respect, and thus their rights routinely, systematically violated. This is just as true when they are used in trivial, duplicative, unnecessary or unwise research as it is when they are used in studies that hold out real promise of human benefits. We can't justify harming or killing a human being just for these sorts of reasons. Neither can we do so even in the case of so lowly a creature as a laboratory rat.

Humans like to think of themselves as the most important and valuable species on earth. Mostly they don't give reasons for this belief, but if pressed might say humans are more intelligent than other animals. We have already seen that intelligence is not what guides our behaviour towards other humans—we don't experiment on the mentally sub-normal. Philosopher Peter Singer points out the contradiction in many people's thinking:

> Why do we lock up chimpanzees in appalling primate research centres and use them in experiments that range from the uncomfortable to the agonising and lethal, yet would never think of doing the same to a retarded human being at a much lower mental level? The only possible answer is that the chimpanzee, no matter how bright, is not human, while the retarded human, no matter how dull, is. This is speciesism pure and simple, and it is as indefensible as the most blatant racism.

Speciesism

The way animals are exploited and treated without respect is a prejudice like racism. It is saying that some individuals don't count simply because they are of a different race (racism), or a different species (speciesism).

Prejudices have changed slowly over the centuries—it is no longer acceptable to say that people of other races, women, or the handicapped don't count. It is also not acceptable to say that animals don't count. As Peter Singer has said:

> *Any being capable of feeling anything, whether pain or pleasure or any kind of positive or negative state of consciousness, must therefore count.*

But if it is wrong to violate the rights of individuals by harming them in experiments, how can the suffering caused by diseases be lessened? Here Peter Singer has said:

> *If in our present situation we find ourselves faced with the dilemma of inflicting harm on an animal in an experiment, or allowing harm from a disease to go unchecked, the best possible solution is to find a way around such a dilemma.*

Medical research would not stop without animals. There is already valuable research going on that doesn't cause harm in the process. . . . This is the way around the ethical dilemma, and the way of the future.

"Human beings experience life, even at its most 'animalistic' level, in a way that fundamentally differs from other creatures."

Animals Are Not Equal to Humans

Damon Linker

Damon Linker contends in the following viewpoint that animals are not equal to humans because they are not moral creatures. Linker attacks the arguments of prominent philosophers within the animal rights movement to support his contentions. He maintains that humans alone are able to differentiate between right and wrong, and he argues that if animals are given equal legal status with people, human life will be demeaned. Damon Linker is an associate editor for *First Things* magazine.

As you read, consider the following questions:
1. According to Linker, what was the result of the October 2000 settlement between the U.S. Department of Agriculture and the Alternatives Research and Development Foundation?
2. What specific human acts does the author describe to illustrate that humans operate on a higher moral plane than do animals?
3. What effect has the animal rights movement had on biomedical research, according to Estelle Fishbein?

From "Rights for Rodents," by Damon Linker, *Commentary*, April 2001.

Not so long ago, animal-rights activists were viewed as crackpots if not thugs, the sort of people who splattered the fur coats of unsuspecting pedestrians with red paint or vandalized university research laboratories. This image was greatly enhanced by the extreme language in which the movement's leading figures routinely expressed themselves. Ingrid Newkirk, the longtime president of People for the Ethical Treatment of Animals (PETA), once opined that "a rat is a pig is a dog is a boy"; on another memorable occasion, she offered the thought that whereas "six million Jews died in concentration camps, . . . six billion broiler chickens will die this year in slaughterhouses."

Expanding Animal Rights

In recent years, however, as some of the movement's most militant groups have moderated their rhetoric and their tactics, the cause of animal rights has begun to achieve a quite astonishing degree of respectability. On Capitol Hill, elected officials from both political parties have become receptive to the movement's concerns, sponsoring legislation and even forming a congressional caucus called the "Friends of Animals." Perhaps even more strikingly, some of the nation's leading law schools, including Harvard, Georgetown, and Rutgers, have begun to offer courses in animal-rights law, and a Washington firm founded by two veterans of Ralph Nader's consumer-advocacy group has begun regularly filing suit to expand legal protections for animals. Its most notable achievement is a landmark federal-court ruling in 1999 that for the first time gives an individual the legal standing to sue on behalf of a distressed creature.

But the biggest victory so far for the animal-rights movement came in October 2000, when the U.S. Department of Agriculture (USDA) agreed to settle a lawsuit filed by a group called the Alternatives Research and Development Foundation that was seeking to expand the scope of the Animal Welfare Act of 1966. Since its passage, this act had been interpreted as empowering the USDA to oversee the treatment in laboratory experiments of large animals like dogs, cats, and primates. Left out of this regulatory regime were birds and, most importantly, mice and rats, which account for 95 percent of all animals used in scientific tests.

Under the October 2000 settlement—and despite the protests of indignant researchers—rodents are now to receive equal rights. The USDA has agreed to require universities, pharmaceutical companies, and other organizations that conduct biomedical experiments to fill out a report on the treatment of each and every warm-blooded animal, and to conduct random inspections to check for conformity to the new standards.

From the eagerness of politicians to please pet-owners to the all-too-familiar activism of the courts, one might point to all sorts of explanations for this dramatic change in the fortunes of the animal-rights movement. But the most basic reason is simpler and more ominous: many Americans have begun to accept the activists' argument that there is a moral imperative to treat animals like, well, people.

Peter Singer

The first leg of this argument concerns the capacity of animals to feel, and the definitive treatment of the question may be found in a book that helped launch the modern animal-rights movement. This was *Animal Liberation* (1975) by Peter Singer, the Australian professor of philosophy who, amid much controversy, was . . . appointed to a prestigious chair in ethics at Princeton.

The power of Singer's book derives largely from the simplicity of its argument. Following the lead of the 19th-century utilitarian philosopher Jeremy Bentham, Singer begins by identifying what he takes to be an indisputable moral intuition: we have an obligation not to inflict pain and suffering on creatures that are capable of experiencing them. Next, using a series of shockingly gory anecdotes, he shows that animals can and do experience these sensations. Finally, and completing his syllogism, he concludes that human beings must not inflict pain and suffering on animals.

Much of Animal Liberation is concerned with applying this principle to various human practices—from the use of animals in scientific experiments to raising and slaughtering them on "factory farms"—and then advocating the radical reformation or abolition of those practices. As Singer writes with characteristic bluntness, "there can be no reason . . . for refusing to extend the basic principle of equality of [ethical] consideration to members of other species." In this scheme, the dominion of humans over animals resembles nothing so much as a "tyranny" based on "arbitrary discrimination."

The Enormous Gulf Between Species

Animal activists . . . remind us of the huge overlap in DNA between human beings and chimpanzees. The fact itself is incontrovertible. Yet the implications we should draw from that fact are not. The observed behavioral differences between humans and chimpanzees are still what they have always been; they are neither increased nor decreased by the number of common genes. The evolutionary biologist should use this evidence to determine when the lines of chimps separated from that of human beings, but the genetic revelation does not establish that chimps and bonobos are able to engage in the abstract thought that would enable them to present on their own behalf the claims for personhood that [animal rights activists] make on their behalf. The number of common genes humans have with other primates is also very high, as it is even with other animals that diverged from human beings long before the arrival of primates. The question to answer is not how many genes humans and chimpanzees have in common; it is how many traits they have in common. The large number of common genes helps explain empirically the rapid rate of evolution. It does not narrow the enormous gulf that a few genes are able to create.

Richard A. Epstein, *The Responsive Community*, Spring 2000.

Indeed, in a parallel that shows up repeatedly in his subsequent writings and those of his many admirers, Singer compares the amount of pain and suffering inflicted on animals to "that which resulted from the centuries of tyranny by white humans over black humans." Just as slavery was based on racism, the abusive treatment of animals rests on what he calls "speciesism"—a prejudice "in favor of the interests of members of one's own species." Those who ignore the suffering of animals rely on the same sort of "difference that the most crude and overt kind of racist uses in attempting to justify racial discrimination."

For Singer, in short, only a complete break from the anthropocentric views of Western philosophy and religion will allow us to see that when it comes to the all-important capacity to experience pleasure and pain, we are morally indistinguishable from many of our fellow creatures.

Steven Wise

Steven Wise's *Rattling the Cage* (2000) is perhaps the best-known book representing a relatively new tack in the project begun by Singer. He, too, offers an anguished cry of protest, again equating the present-day treatment of animals with human enslavement and describing the use of animals for medical research as "genocide." But for Wise, who teaches the new course in animal-rights law at Harvard and is a tireless courtroom advocate for the cause, the essential similarity between men and (some) beasts is autonomy: that is, the shared ability to form preferences and act on them.

Scientists, Wise points out, have demonstrated important physiological parallels between human beings and the primates that are his chief concern in *Rattling the Cage*. Chimpanzees, for instance, not only share 98.3 percent of our genetic make-up, but they have similar brain structures as well. On the evidence of evolutionary theory, he declares, "as recently as 5 or 6 million years ago, humans, chimpanzees, and bonobos were the same animal."

As a result, Wise argues, chimpanzees and bonobos possess myriad attributes that, through a combination of ignorance and prideful prejudice, we normally associate solely with human beings. They "feel" and "think," exhibit "emotions" and live in "cultures," "understand cause-and-effect relationships among objects, and even relationships among relationships." More importantly, observation of these animals in captivity and in the wild reveals that their behavior echoes ours in striking ways. They seem to possess elementary self-awareness: they imitate one another, engage in deception and trickery, and use their own primitive languages to communicate basic information and emotional states. A chimpanzee named Lucy even regularly prepared tea for researchers and masturbated to pictures of naked men in *Playgirl* magazine.

Contrary to Western prejudices that trace back to the Bible and Aristotle, Wise concludes, animals—or at least chimpanzees and bonobos—are not simply "things" that can be treated as property. They are, instead, "persons" in the legal sense. Like us, that is, they are bearers of individual rights and deserve to be treated accordingly. As the renowned primatologist Jane Goodall puts it in her glowing foreword to *Rattling the Cage*, this book is meant to be the animals' "Magna Carta [which in 1215 outlined English civil liberties], [the U.S.] Declaration of Independence, and [the United Nations] Universal Declaration of [Human] Rights all in one."

Science Ignores Morality

That such arguments have found an audience at this particular cultural moment is not so hard to explain. Our popular and elite media are saturated with scientific and quasi-scientific reports claiming to prove the basic thesis of the animal-rights movement. Having once believed ourselves to be made in the image of God, we now learn—from the human genome project, the speculations of evolutionary psychologists, and numerous other sources—that humankind, too, is determined by genetic predispositions and the drive to reproduce. We are cleverer than other animals, to be sure, but the difference is one of degree, not of kind. As Verlyn Klinkenborg recently wrote on the editorial page of the *New York Times*, "Again and again, after starting from an ancient premise of radical differences between humans and other creatures, scientists have discovered profound similarities."

But have they? Genetics and evolutionary biology may be, indeed, extremely effective at identifying the traits we share with other species. But chemistry, for its part, can tell us about the ways in which we resemble chunks of charcoal, and physics can point to fundamental similarities between a man and all the matter in the universe. The problem with these observations is not that they are untrue. It is that they shed no light whatsoever on, or rather they are designed to obfuscate, what makes humanity unique as a species—the point on which an answer to the likes of Peter Singer and Steven Wise must hinge.

For his part, Singer commits the same error that philosopher John Stuart Mill found in the system of Jeremy Bentham: he makes no distinction among kinds of pleasure and pain. That animals feel emotions can hardly be doubted; but human beings experience life, even at its most "animalistic" level, in a way that fundamentally differs from other creatures.

Thus, Singer can account for the pain that humans and animals alike experience when they are hungry and the pleasure they feel when they eat, but he cannot explain, for example, a person's choice to starve himself for a cause. He understands that human beings, like animals, derive pleasure from sex and sometimes endure pangs of longing when they are deprived of it, but he cannot explain how or why, unlike animals, some choose to embrace celibacy for the sake of its noble purity. He is certainly attuned to the tendency we share with animals to fear and avoid pain and bodily harm, but he is incapable of understanding a man's willingness to face certain death on the battlefield when called upon to do so by his country. Still less can he explain why stories of such sacrifice sometimes move us to tears.

In much the same way, the evidence adduced by Steven Wise to suggest that primates are capable of forming rudimentary plans and expectations fails to demonstrate they are equal to human beings in any significant sense. Men and women use their "autonomy" in a world defined not by the simple imperatives of survival but by ideas of virtue and vice, beauty and ugliness, right and wrong. Modern scientific methods, including those of evolutionary psychology, have so far proved incapable of detecting and measuring this world, but that does not make any less real the experience that takes place within it.

Western civilization has tended to regard animals as resembling things more than human beings precisely because, like inanimate objects, and unlike the authors of the real Magna Carta, animals have no perception of morality. Until the day when a single animal stands up and, led by a love of justice and a sense of self-worth, insists that the world recognize and respect its dignity, all the philosophical gyrations of the activists will remain so much sophistry.

Biomedical Research

None of this, of course, exempts human beings from behaving decently toward animals, but it does provide a foundation, when necessary, for giving pride of place to the interests of human beings. This has particular relevance for biomedical research.

Among the most vociferous critics of the USDA's recent capitulation to the animal-rights movement were the nation's leading centers of medical science. The National Association for Biomedical Research estimated that the new regulations would cost universities alone as much as $280 million a year. Nor is the issue simply one of dollars. As Estelle Fishbein, counsel for Johns Hopkins University, recently argued in the *Journal of the American Medical Association*,

> Genetic research promises to bring new therapies to alleviate human suffering from the acquired immunodeficiency syndrome, Parkinson's disease and other neurological diseases, and virtually all other human and animal diseases. However, the promise of this new era of medical research is highly dependent on the ready availability of mice, rats, and birds.

Far from being a mere administrative hassle, she concluded, the new regulations would "divert scarce grant funds from actual research use, distract researchers from their scientific work, and overload them with documentation requirements."

Serious as this threat is, a still more troubling one is the effect that the arguments of animal-rights proponents may have, in the long term, on our regard for human life itself. Peter Singer's appointment at Princeton caused a stir not because of his writings about animals but because of his endorsement of euthanasia, unrestricted abortion, and, in some instances, infanticide. But all of his views, as he himself maintains, are of a piece. The idea that "human infants and retarded adults" are superior to animals can only be based, he writes, on "a bare-faced—and morally indefensible—prejudice for members of our own species."

In much the same way, Steven Wise urges us to reject absolute demarcations between species and instead focus on the capacities of individual humans and individual apes. If we do that, we will find that many adult chimpanzees and bonobos are far more "human" than newborn and mentally disabled human beings, and thus just as worthy of being recognized as "persons."

Though Wise's inference is the opposite of Singer's—he

does not wish to deprive underdeveloped humans of rights so much as to extend those rights to primates—he is playing the same game of bait-and-switch: in this case projecting the noblest human attributes onto animals while quietly limiting his sample of human beings to newborns and the mentally disabled. When raising animals to our level proves to be impossible, as it inevitably must, equal consideration can only be won by attempting to lower us to theirs.

Human Prejudice Benefits All

It is a curious fact that in virtually all of human history, only in liberal democracies—societies founded on the recognition of the innate dignity of all members of the human race—have animals enjoyed certain minimum protections, codified in our own country in the Animal Welfare Act. It is a no less curious fact that these same liberal democracies have become infected over the past decades with a corrosive self-doubt, giving rise in some educated circles to antiliberal, antiwhite, antimale, anti-Western, and now, with perfect logic, antihuman enthusiasms.

The proponents of these various but linked ideologies march under a banner of justice and the promise of extending the blessings of equality to one or more excluded Others. Such piety is to be expected in a radical movement seeking well-meaning allies; but it need not deflect us from the main focus of their aggressive passions, which the euthanasia-endorsing Peter Singer, for one, has at least had the candor to admit to. Can anyone really doubt that, were the misanthropic agenda of the animal-rights movement actually to succeed, the result would be an increase in man's inhumanity, to man and animal alike? In the end, fostering our age-old "prejudice" in favor of human dignity may be the best thing we can do for animals, not to mention for ourselves.

| "The animal rights message of compassion and respect resonates with the core ethical teaching of each of the world's major religions."

Core Teachings of the World's Religions Support Animal Rights

Norm Phelps

Norm Phelps is Spiritual Outreach Director for The Fund for Animals, an organization that works for animal rights. In the following viewpoint, Phelps claims that animal rights activists should persuade those in the religious community to support animal rights. He believes activists can succeed in doing so because the core ethical teachings of the world's major religions agree with the tenets of the animal rights movement. Although the doctrines of most religions appear to deny equal standing to animals, Phelps argues that those doctrines are often misrepresented or violate core religious teachings.

As you read, consider the following questions:
1. What four reasons does Phelps give for engaging religious communities on the side of animal rights?
2. According to the author, what is "the alpha and omega" of animal rights?
3. What is the first and overriding precept of Buddhism, according to Phelps?

Historically, the animal rights movement has been hesitant about starting a dialogue with organized religion. While individual advocates often work to recruit their co-believers to the side of the animals (Andrew Linzey in Christianity, Richard Schwartz in Judaism, and Philip Kapleau in Buddhism jump to mind), as a movement we have seemed unwilling to approach religious communities on behalf of nonhuman animals.

Reasons to Engage Religion

I am sure this is largely because one of the tacit rules of our society is that we don't question or criticize someone else's religious beliefs—it just isn't polite. Also, some activists may feel inadequately prepared to discuss animal rights in a religious context, while others may find it more urgent to focus on institutions that are actually committing the most egregious animal abuse. We tell ourselves that social movements on behalf of women's rights and gay/lesbian rights have made important progress without the religious community, so why can't we? The reason is that animal rights differs from other social reform movements in four ways that make engaging religious communities on the side of the animals essential to our success.

First, no social reformers in history have attempted to restructure society on the scale that we are undertaking. Human civilization, in all its forms, is so intertwined with animal exploitation that the concept of animal rights represents the most profound reorganization of society since the invention of agriculture and the creation of cities.

Second, animal rights is the only social movement in history whose beneficiaries cannot participate in it and whose participants cannot benefit from it. Other reform movements have been able to draw their primary momentum—and their continuity and perseverance when the going gets tough—from the population that would benefit from success. We can't do that.

Third, most Americans believe that their quality of life depends upon animal exploitation. Julia Child was recently quoted as saying that she felt sorry for vegetarians, because when they sit down to the table they never have anything to look forward to. That's nonsense, but the great majority of Americans believe it, just as they believe that their health and safety depend on vivisection and their family life would suffer without trips to the circus and the zoo. Most of our friends and neighbors are convinced that their lives would be less safe, less comfortable, and less enjoyable if animal exploitation came to an end. To their way of thinking, we are asking them to make sacrifices that are of no benefit to themselves or their loved ones.

Finally, when we first admit the justice of the animals' cause, we come up against the reality that our way of life violates, on a daily basis, the most basic moral principles. Faced with that recognition, most people go into hard denial and stay there.

The Alpha and Omega of Animal Rights

In short, animal activists are telling people something they very much do not want to hear. We are asking them to give up comforts and pleasures that they have enjoyed all their lives, to launch society into an uncharted realm, and in the process to face the fact that their lifestyles have been built on practices that are morally indefensible. And we are asking them to do all of this simply because it is the right thing to do. In the final analysis, the argument for animal rights is entirely an ethical argument.

It is wrong for humankind to inflict suffering and premature death on sentient creatures because we enjoy the taste of their flesh, think their skin looks good on our feet, hope that if we torture and kill enough of them we may live to be 100, or whatever. That is the alpha and the omega of animal rights. There may be other, entirely valid reasons for doing things that advance the animals' cause—such as adopting a vegan lifestyle to improve our health, or eliminating animal agriculture to benefit the environment and end world hunger—but there is no reason other than ethics for granting animals rights.

Radiating Influence

It so happens that there is a vast worldwide network of organizations that have as one of their primary purposes the teaching and promotion of ethical behavior: religious communities. Not only do they enjoy a massive membership, but they have a radiating influence that permeates the entire culture. In public behavior and private morality, they play a major role in setting the moral and ethical tone of society. If activists are going to persuade the public to give up the supposed benefits of animal exploitation for altruistic reasons, we will need the moral authority of organized religion (or at least a large portion of it) behind us. We must therefore enlist religious communities on the side of animal rights. Although this will be neither quick nor easy—most religions are not noted for the ease and rapidity with which they embrace change—it can be done.

Treat Animals as God Intends

The creation waits with eager longing for the revealing of the sons of God. And who are these? They are, simply put, Spirit-led individuals who will make possible a new order of existence; who will show by their life the possibility of newness of life. Quite practically the task required of us is to recognize God's rights in his creation, rights for animals to be themselves as God intends: to life; to be free; and to live without suffering, distress and injury.

Andrew Linzey, *Christianity and the Rights of Animals*, 1987.

All of the world's major religions build their ethics on the same foundation: boundless love and compassion for others. In Jainism, for example, this is expressed in the teaching that *ahimsa paramo dharma*: "Harmlessness is the highest law." The most revered sage in modern Hinduism, Mahatma Gandhi, taught that *ahimsa* (nonviolence, harmlessness) is the foundation of all moral action. In Buddhism, the first and overriding precept is "Do not kill," which is taken to mean, "Do not harm any living being." The *suras* of the Koran begin, "In the name of Allah, the Merciful, the Compassionate," thereby establishing mercy and compassion as prime attributes of divinity. Hillel the Great affirmed that the essence of Jewish ethics is to "love your neighbor as yourself," while Jesus made the same affirmation the basis of Christian ethics.

How Animal Rights and Religion Intersect

The animal rights message of compassion and respect resonates with the core ethical teaching of each of the world's major religions. Unfortunately, all except Jainism also contain doctrines or practices that limit the ethical consideration accorded animals. In these cases our task, to quote Albert Schweitzer, is to persuade the religious communities to "expand the circle of [their] compassion to include all living beings." There is no need to convince anyone to change their fundamental belief, simply to enlarge the application of a belief they already hold—a much easier task.

To put it another way, the harmony between the fundamental principle of animal rights and the fundamental ethical teachings of the world's major religions creates the opportunity for us to demonstrate that traditions—even scriptural ones—that appear to deny moral standing to animals have either been subjected to misinterpretation or violate the core ethical teaching of the religion. Animal rights is the logical conclusion to which the basic ethical doctrines of the world religions lead us.

We all recognize that this will not be a quick or easy undertaking. Organized religions sometimes demonstrate a considerable resistance to change and a notable ability to rationalize contradictions within their own teachings. Witness the record on full participation for women and homosexuals. But for the animals, it is both a necessary endeavor and one that can lead to success, provided that with patience, respect, and persistence, we keep directing the dialogue to the resonating principle of unbounded compassion.

As a tactical matter, it can be valuable for activists who are religious to work within their own communities; in the minds of many, their membership will lend them credibility. But animal rights as a movement, and secular animal rights organizations, need to reach out to religious communities without concern for denominational affinity. It is in no way necessary to practice a particular religion, or any religion at all, to engage its followers in a dialogue on behalf of animal rights. Compassion is a universal value that everyone has standing to defend.

For too long, we have paid too little attention to religious communities. In the words of Cleveland Amory, animal activists take on the responsibility of "speaking for those who can't," and the time has come for us to speak to the churches and synagogues, to the mosques, mandiras [Hindu temples], and meditation centers. We have a message that they need to hear, and a cause they need to take for their own.

"The fact that animals may be used in scientific procedures for the benefit of people shows that [Christians] believe that human beings have more value than animals."

The World's Major Religions Support Animal Experimentation

Seriously Ill for Medical Research

Seriously Ill for Medical Research (SIMR) is a patients' group formed to voice support for humane research into human diseases. In the following viewpoint, the organization contends that all of the world's major religions believe that human life is more valuable than animal life, and therefore condone animal experimentation for human benefit. The organization notes that most religions also stress that animal testing be conducted as humanely as possible, and points out that laws in Great Britain already guarantee the welfare of animals used in research.

As you read, consider the following questions:

1. According to Seriously Ill for Medical Research, what do the world's religions mean by "dominion"?
2. What are Quaker doctors who hold Home Office licenses permitted to do, according to the organization?
3. What is the first precept in Buddhism, according to the organization?

Excerpted from "The Major Religions on Animals and Medical Research," by Seriously Ill for Medical Research, www.simr.org.uk, 1994. Copyright © 1994 by Seriously Ill for Medical Research. Reprinted with permission.

The use of animals for medical research is a complex scientific and moral issue. It is easy to point to the scientific and medical benefits that have been gained using animals, but this does not resolve the unease that many people and researchers feel about whether it is morally right to take the life of animals in pursuit of scientific knowledge and better medical treatments. Many people gain their moral values from the organised religions and even secular people would find it impossible to deny the importance of religion to the social and political lives of most countries.

Sometimes a religious standpoint is clearly given in the holy books, sometimes an interpretation or official pronouncement is made by a religious leader based on a written passage. It is noteworthy that, while all religions recognise the importance of animals in the world, none of the world's major religions holds ceremonies to mark the birth or death of animals. This point emphasises the relative importance placed on animal life compared to human life by the major religions. Nonetheless, the morality of the use of animals is an important issue, and the world's religions consider that it lies properly within their domain.

The views of the world's great religions on the use of animal experimentation for scientific purposes need to be brought to the attention of both scientists and animal protection groups.

Major Religious Tenets

Broadly, the major religions all propose the following points:
- That human life is more valuable than animal life. From the religious perspective this is based on the belief that humans are uniquely responsible and capable of salvation. This is quite different from the philosophical view that human life is more valuable because humans are more aware of pain and pleasure
- That humans have a God-given authority over other animals. Usually expressed as 'dominion' or 'stewardship' it implies a position of trust and also responsibility
- It is recognised that humans eat animals and use them for other reasons such as work. The right to do these things is enshrined in most religions

- That cruelty to animals is to be abhorred because it displays attributes that are undesirable in civilised societies
- By this is meant pointless acts that will cause an animal to experience pain or suffering. Besides the previous point which condemns cruelty, most religions positively urge kindness towards animals.

Church of England

A key reference in the New Testament on this topic is Matthew 10 vv. 29–31. All the Christian denominations take this as a starting point.

A man is worth many sparrows, but not one sparrow can die unnoticed in God's World.

The Church of England has specifically made statements about the relationships between humankind and animals. Mostly these predate the 1986 Animals (Scientific Procedures) Act and arose from consultation between the church and the government.

The fact that animals may be used in scientific procedures for the benefit of people shows that we believe that human beings have more value than animals. But the fact that we minimise the pain, suffering, distress or lasting harm that animals may have to undergo shows that we regard them as having intrinsic value.

Baptists

The Social Affairs office of the Baptist church in a private communication says:

Most Baptists would be sympathetic to the use of animals in medical research, but less enthusiastic about their use in cosmetic products.

Methodism

The Methodist church has issued a statement on the subject of the treatment of animals.

It should be horrifying that millions of animals are killed every year in laboratory experiments, but most of them have been bred for the purpose and the outcome of the experimentation is valuable advance in both human and veterinary medicine.

Unnecessary or unjustifiable experimentation, as on the effect of cosmetics; the use of numbers of animals in an experiment far in excess of a reasonable control and check number; excessive duplication of experiments in different laboratories; the use of animals when valid results could be secured from tissue cultures; are all to be condemned.

Some of these requirements are exactly those of the current controls on medical research involving animals in Britain. The Animals (Scientific Procedures) Act 1986 states, among other things, that all such procedures require a licence that provides evidence of the need to perform those procedures, and that no licence will be issued if there is any valid alternative to using animals.

Quakers

There is no tradition of authoritative statements from the organising body of Quakers, according to Beth Smith, General Secretary of Quaker Social Responsibility and Education. She goes as far as to say:

> *The most controversial area of animal exploitation for Quakers is that of medical experimentation. There are many Quaker doctors and some medical researchers who hold Home Office licences to experiment on live animals. The latter would justify their actions by citing the beneficial results which they feel can be achieved for humans and animals through the knowledge gained.*

Quakers prefer to allow the individual members to come to their own conclusions about the morality of animal experimentation, but they are generally tolerant towards those individuals who do support it.

Catholicism

An interpretation of the Catholic Catechism is offered by Nicholas Coote, the Assistant General Secretary of the Catholic Bishop's Conference of England and Wales. He stresses that the Catechism should be seen only as a starting point for further discussion.

> *Provided they remain within reasonable limits medical and scientific experiments on animals are morally acceptable since they may help to save human lives or advance therapy.*

At the 5th International Conference on the Brain and Mind, the Pope himself emphasised the importance of medical research to benefit humankind.

> *My praise and encouragement, then, go out to all of you—scientists, doctors, researchers, scholars, and pastors of souls who devote your-*

selves with impassioned commitment to studying the very noble and profound subject of the human mind. . . . The boundless field of the neurosciences—from neurobiology to neurochemistry, from psychosomatic medicine to psychoendocrinology—offers research the possibility of approaching in a particularly penetrating way the threshold of the very mystery of man.

Judaism

Judaism recognises that animal experimentation holds many benefits for humankind and animals.

Isserles (Ramah) states that anything necessary for medical or other useful purposes is excluded from the prohibition of cruelty to animals.

Rabbi John D Rayner, Chairman of the Council of Reform and Liberal Rabbis, offers this quotation from 'What Does Judaism Say About . . ?' by Rabbi Dr Peter Jacobs.

A very good case can be made out for vivisection of animals provided safeguards are taken to reduce the pain to a minimum. Here the benefits to medical progress are considerable and the price worth paying.

Rabbi Rayner himself adds:

[I] would regard any experimentation on animals as ethically permissible provided (a) that it is done in such a way as to cause the least possible suffering to the animals and (b) that there is real basis for the hope that such experimentation may lead to the saving of human life or the relief of human suffering.

Indeed, I would be inclined to add a further condition namely that authority to permit such experimentation should be vested in an ethics committee composed of persons who have no interest in the

---

Animal Rights Movement Is Anti-Christian

Our contemporary animal rights movement is heir to a long tradition of trying to narrow the gap between humans and lower animals. But what motive lies behind this tradition? The answer seems obvious enough. Specifically, the motive is anti-Christian; more generally, it is a strong animosity toward the view of human nature taken both by biblical religions and by the great classical schools of philosophy, especially Platonism and Stoicism. That man is "made in the image and likeness of God" is an expression found in the Bible, but it is a formula that well expresses the anthropology of Plato and the Stoics as well. To reduce human nature to nothing more than its biological status is to attack this ancient and exalted conception of human nature.

David R. Carlin, *First Things*, August 2000.

---

potential commercial value of any pharmaceutical products that may be [the] result from such experimentation.

The Animals (Scientific Procedures) Act requires that painkillers and anaesthetics are used whenever necessary, and that veterinary attention should be available to animals used in medical research. Furthermore, licences are granted (or refused) by Home Office Inspectors who have no commercial interest in the products of animal procedures. A separate advisory committee, the Animal Procedures Committee, advises the Home Secretary.

Islam

An interpretation of the statements about animals in the Qur'an is given by the author and Qur'anic scholar Al Hafiz B A Masri:

> *Some research on animals may yet be justified, given the traditions of Islam. Basic and applied research in the biological and social sciences, for example, will be allowed, if the laboratory animals are not caused pain or disfigured, and if human beings or other animals would benefit because of the research.*

> *Actions shall be judged according to intention. Any kind of medical treatment of animals and experiments on them becomes ethical and legal or unethical and illegal according to the intention of the person who does it.*

Hinduism and Sikhism

Hinduism and its close relative, Sikhism, are different from Judaism, Christianity or Islam in that they have no 'bible' or 'rule book' giving instruction. The sacred texts, for example, the Sri Isopanisad, require some interpretation by the reader or a priest. Any quotes from Hindu religious writings should be read with this in mind. There are many ways in which Hinduism or Sikhism may be practised and this can vary greatly between communities and individuals.

There are central tenets to the Hindu faith most notably the belief in reincarnation, sometimes as an animal. All animal life is revered because in the eyes of a Hindu all animals are the receptacles of souls. Consequently, Hindus have a general aim to be vegetarian, but many are not. There are also many Hindu doctors and medical researchers who use animals in research.

Any decision about the morality of animal experiments is left to the individual. While some followers of Hinduism would not choose to perform animal experiments, most would be tolerant of it because of its value to humans and animals.

One interpretation of the Sri Isopanisads is given by His Divine Grace A C Bhaktivedanta Swami Prabhupada, writing on the subject of animals:

> *A human life is distinguished from animal life due to its heavy responsibilities. . . . The human being is given all facilities for a comfortable life by the laws of nature because the human form of life is more important and valuable than animal life. . . . As human beings we are not meant for simply solving economic problems on a tottering platform but for solving all the problems of the material life into which we have been placed by the laws of nature.*

This extract comments upon the burdens placed upon humankind by virtue of being different from animals. According to the text these differences impose a duty on humankind to solve all the problems of the material life. This must logically include curing diseases, those most material of problems, and presumably acknowledges any reasonable use of animals in this respect.

Buddhism

Buddhism draws largely from Hinduism. The most devout— Zen Buddhists—believe that all life is sacred. More ordinary Buddhists will probably admit the necessity of taking animal life under certain circumstances. The Buddhist standpoint is embodied in the first Precept:

> *I undertake the rule of training not to do any harm to any living (breathing) thing.*

This precept implies something more than simply not harming living things. It includes actively helping people or animals suffering from misfortune or disease and this process may involve the use of animals. In a personal communication, Ronald C Maddox, General Secretary of The Buddhist Society, says:

> *All of us, it has to be admitted, have probably benefited in some measure from animal experiments and their suffering. Some Buddhists may up to a point be willing to accept this in the interests of humanity. Others may themselves reject this and be fully willing to forego any potential benefits.*

"Will radicals rule and research aimed at saving human life suffer far more than the animals?"

Animal Rights Activists Are Terrorists

Cal Thomas

In the following viewpoint, Cal Thomas argues that animal rights activists are dangerous because they use violence to further their cause. Thomas maintains that animal rights activists often finance high-profile terrorist acts that do little to help animals instead of donating money to animal shelters where thousands of pets die each year. He contends that these activists have put human health in jeopardy by attacking labs where vital biomedical research is conducted. Cal Thomas is a nationally syndicated columnist.

As you read, consider the following questions:
1. How much more did People for the Ethical Treatment of Animals spend on activist Rodney Coronado's defense than on animal shelters in 1992?
2. How many instances of animal rights violence have occurred in the United States, according to the Justice Department?
3. Why does Thomas think animal rights activist Paul McCartney is a hypocrite?

Excerpted from "Animals Rights Ambuscade," by Cal Thomas, *Washington Times*, June 22, 1997. Copyright © Tribune Media Services. Reprinted with permission.

A coalition of animal rights groups opens a five-day convention in Washington in June 1997 to promote their view that animals should have at least as many rights as humans and that using them in scientific experiments to find cures for human diseases is cruel and must be outlawed.

Violence on Behalf of Animals

If that was all there was to it, then People for the Ethical Treatment of Animals (PETA), the Humane Society of the U.S. (HSUS) and their fellow neighers and cluckers could be dismissed as just one more interest group trying to win attention from Congress and the press. But these people have condoned violence to advance their cause.

In testimony before a House Appropriations subcommittee on March 12, 1997, FBI Director Louis Freeh noted the extent of special interest terrorist activity. He cited as one example a Feb. 2, 1992, arson of the mink research facility at Michigan State University. Rodney Coronado, a member of the Animal Liberation Front, pleaded guilty and was sentenced to 57 months in prison. PETA sent $45,200 to Coronado's "support committee," which was a sum 15 times greater than what PETA spent on animal shelters nationwide in all of that year.

The attack on the lab interfered with toxicology research designed, among other things, to help not only humans but to improve the quality of marine life in Lake Huron.

The Justice Department says there have been more than 313 instances of animal rights violence in the United States. This has led to a research-cost increase of between 10 percent and 20 percent, much of it funded by taxpayers.

While PETA and the other groups loudly condemn scientific research involving animals (90 percent of which are rodents, according to Americans for Medical Progress, a pro-research foundation), they spend a pittance on animal shelters. Eleven million animals are destroyed annually for lack of facilities. Yet PETA spent less than $3,955 of its $12 million in fiscal 1995 and $6,100 of its $10.9 million in fiscal 1996 for shelter programs, according to its nonprofit tax forms filed with the Internal Revenue Service. The HSUS does not operate a single shelter, despite a $40 million budget.

Celebrity Extremists

Animal rights groups want us to believe all research involving any animal is cruel and unnecessary. Some have the attitude of actor Alec Baldwin who told KCAL-TV during PETA's Los Angeles gala on December 14, 1997, that we don't need animal research because there are "a lot of human subjects who would be more than willing to become live experiments."

Just how absurd are some animal rights people about their cause? Ex-Beatle Paul McCartney is leading a campaign against the March of Dimes because it works with animals in research. But Mr. McCartney's wife, Linda, is taking chemotherapy treatment for breast cancer that was developed through animal research, mostly on fruit flies, mice and rats.

'You're right. I was a fool to have given in to those damned animal-rights activists.'

Jones. © 2000 by *The Spectator*. Reprinted with permission.

The language is far more extreme than anything said by Operation Rescue in its attempts to stop human abortions. Many politicians and the media viewed that organization as dangerous.

Ingrid Newkirk, founder of PETA, once told the *Washington Post*, "Six million Jews died in concentration camps, but six billion broiler chickens will die this year in slaughterhouses."

Alex Pacheco, chairman of PETA, told the *New York Times*, "We feel that animals have the same rights as a retarded human child because they are equal mentally in terms of dependence on others." Mr. Pacheco added: "Arson, property destruction, burglary and theft are 'acceptable crimes' when used for the animal cause."

Political scientist Kevin Beedy, writing in the March 1990 issue of *Animals' Agenda*, said: "Terrorism carries no moral or ethical connotations. It is simply the definition of a particular type of coercion. It is up to the animal rights spokespersons either to dismiss the terrorist label as propaganda or make it a badge to be proud of wearing."

This is the crowd that is coming to Washington. Group yoga sessions lead off each day. Meals will be strictly vegetarian. Will radicals rule and research aimed at saving human life suffer far more than the animals?

| *"Violence has not characterized the animal rights movement."*

Animal Rights Activists Are Not Terrorists

Jane Cartmill

Jane Cartmill is the director of San Diego Animal Advocates, an organization that works to protect the welfare of animals. In the following viewpoint, Cartmill contends that critics of animal rights activists unfairly characterize the animal rights movement as violent. She argues that the perpetrators of violence are actually the humans who work in slaughterhouses, factory farms, and biomedical research labs.

As you read, consider the following questions:

1. How does Cartmill refute the claim that there have been 313 violent acts committed by animal rights activists?
2. List three examples provided by the author to illustrate institutionalized brutality against animals.
3. Name three ways that animals are used for biomedical research, according to the author.

Excerpted from "Animals Are Victims of Violence," by Jane Cartmill, *San Diego North County Times*, June 29, 1997. Copyright © 1997 by Jane Cartmill. Reprinted with permission.

Columnist Cal Thomas accuses the animal rights movement of condoning violence as a means to achieve its goals. He referred to the Justice Department's list of 313 instances of animal rights violence. What he failed to mention was that the list consists largely of acts of vandalism and unsubstantiated reports of threats.

Violence Against Animals

If a facility wall was spray-painted with a slogan, this would be listed as an act of violence. If a researcher or furrier claimed to have received a menacing phone call, it's on the list. If, in truth, there had been 313 violent acts, there would be dozens of animal rights activists in prison. There aren't, because violence has not characterized the animal rights movement, and no one—other than the activists themselves—has ever been injured in an animal rights action.

But since Mr. Thomas is so very concerned about violence, perhaps he would be willing to take a look at where it really exists—inside the slaughterhouses, research labs, fur "ranches," circuses, rodeos and factory farms.

Let him witness the realities of the widespread and institutionalized brutality against other creatures. He could begin with the bloody clubbing of seals for their pelts; the mangled limbs in the steel-jaw traps; the frantic thrashing of netted whales and dolphins; the searing blade of the debeaking iron [used to keep factory hens from pecking each other to death]; the brain-bashing jolt of the captive bolt pistol [used to kill cows before butchering]; the stagger in agony of a deer wounded by a bowhunter's arrow; the calf or steer slamming to the ground in a roping event; the electric prod forcing a sick and weakened cow into the transport truck; the blown-off face of the sea lion who pestered fishermen; the circular saw slicing the head off a conscious chicken suspended by its feet; dogs hung by the neck and cats boiled alive for foreign fare delicacies; the repeated taunting and spearing of a dying bull in the ring; or the bullets from the muzzle-loader tearing into the flesh of the bear and bison. Just for starters.

And as for that lifesaving medical research, Mr. Thomas might want to observe the force-feeding of toxic chemicals

Composite Animal Rights Activist Profile

Characteristic	OSU%*	USU%*
Sex		
Male	31.6	21.7
Female	68.4	78.3
Age		
29 and under	41.9	23.2
30 to 49	48.0	56.6
50 and over	6.4	20.0
Race		
White	92.9	96.9
Nonwhite	7.1	3.1
Education		
High school diploma, GED, or less	12.3	17.9
Bachelor's degree or some college	40.2	48.4
Some graduate school	7.1	NA
Graduate/professional degree	18.7	33.3
Income		
$19,999 or less	19.0	18.4
$20,000 to $49,999	46.1	42.5
$50,000 or more	18.7	38.9
Residence		
Urban (over 10,000 population)	85.0	73.4
Rural	10.0	26.6
Don't know/Did not answer	5.0	NA
Occupation		
Professional, business, or executive status	44.0	46.0

*OSU=Oregon State University Study, 1990
*USU=Utah State University Study, 1990

Harold D. Guither, *Animal Rights: History and Scope of a Radical Social Movement*, 1998.

to fully conscious rats, rabbits and dogs and their hours of agonized cries; the chemical and mechanical induction of heart attacks and brain hemorrhages in dogs; the blow-torching and scalding of fully-conscious pigs and beagles;

the blinding of fetal monkeys still inside the womb and their subsequent decapitation immediately after birth (currently funded at Salk Institute [a highly respected biomedical research institute]); the electroshocking of primates to force them to use surgically paralyzed limbs; the rabbits in body restraints with chemically burned and blistered eyes; the unrelieved hours of nausea and vomiting from induced radiation poisoning; dogs implanted with rectal probes and placed in microwave ovens to induce heatstroke; infant monkeys in a pit of darkness for a decades-old deprivation study that continues to this day; and the withdrawal throes of rodents and primates forcibly addicted to, and then denied, cocaine, amphetamines and narcotics.

Thomas questions a future in which "radicals" (such as Paul McCartney and Alec Baldwin) rule. He fears the animal rights "crowd" that will convene in Washington, D.C., in June 1997. Just what exactly is he smoking? The radicals and terrorists clearly rule now. The crowd he ought to fear is the one that shamelessly inflicts an almost incomprehensible level of savagery on Earth's animals and considers it normal. These are the true acts of violence.

Periodical Bibliography

The following articles have been selected to supplement the diverse views presented in this chapter. Addresses are provided for periodicals not indexed in the *Readers' Guide to Periodical Literature*, the *Alternative Press Index*, the *Social Sciences Index*, or the *Index to Legal Periodicals and Books*.

James Burnett	"Monkeys in the Middle," *George*, September 2000.
Marianna R. Burt	"Animals as Property: A Two-Edged Sword," *Animal Issues*, Winter 1998.
David R. Carlin	"Rights, Animal and Human," *First Things*, August 2000.
Richard A. Epstein	"The Next Rights Revolution? It's Bowser's Time at Last," *National Review*, November 8, 1999.
Michael Allen Fox	"The Case Against Animal Experimentation," *Organization and Environment*, December 2000.
William Greenway	"Animals and the Love of God," *Christian Century*, June 21–28, 2000.
John F. Kavanaugh	"Being Human," *America*, April 26, 1997.
Gina Kolata	"Tough Tactics in One Battle over Animals in the Lab," *New York Times*, March 24, 1998.
Clay Lancaste	"Worship Versus Investigation: Practices of Religion and Science," *Animals' Agenda*, July/August 1998.
Adrian R. Morrison	"Science and Self-Doubt," *Reason*, October 2000.
Dan Seligman	"Animal Spirits," *Forbes*, May 31, 1999.
Freeman Wicklund	"Direct Action: Progress, Peril, or Both?" *Animals' Agenda*, July/August 1998.
Joy Williams	"The Inhumanity of the Animal People," *Harper's*, August 1997.
Clive Wynne	"Do Animals Think?" *Psychology Today*, December 1, 1999.

CHAPTER 2

Is Animal Experimentation Justified?

Chapter Preface

High school student Jenifer Graham refused to dissect a frog in her biology class, declaring that dissection went against her ethical principles. Dissection—the process of cutting into and studying dead animals—has come increasingly under attack in recent years.

Animal dissection is practiced in high school and college biology classrooms as a way to provide students with hands-on learning experiences with anatomy. Dogs, cats, fish, and fetal pigs are used in dissection, but frogs are used most often. Proponents of dissection argue that it teaches students about organs and circulatory systems better than textbooks can. Dissection advocates in medical schools contend that the practice is the only way to provide students with practice in surgical techniques without risking human lives. High school biology teacher Susan Offner contends that "no model, no video, no diagram and no movie can duplicate the fascination, the sense of discovery, wonder and even awe that students feel when they find real structures in their own specimens."

Opponents of dissection disagree with Offner's contentions. They argue that students can use alternatives such as computer programs or human cadavers to learn about anatomy. Those opposed to dissection claim that many animal specimens such as fish and frogs are taken from the wild, which disrupts the delicate balance of their native habitats. Opponents' most vocal criticism of dissection, however, is that killing animals is a counterproductive way to teach students—especially medical students—to value life. Biology professor George Russell contends that "when life itself is treated as a kind of mechanism to be disassembled, both literally and in thought, an experience of the living whole and the regard and interest that it can inspire are no longer possible."

The debate about dissection is merely part of a larger debate about animal experimentation. In the following chapter, doctors and animal rights activists argue whether animal experimentation is justified. As school starts each year, thousands of first-time biology students will be asked to dissect an animal and will have to weigh for themselves the pros and cons of animal experimentation.

> "*If we insist upon granting rights to humans we should also grant them to animals. Animal experimentation then becomes illegitimate.*"

Animal Experimentation Is Unethical

Robert Garner

Robert Garner is a reader in politics at the University at Leicester, England, and has published widely on animal rights and environmental politics. In the following viewpoint, Garner asserts that animals have a higher moral status than society has traditionally granted them, which makes animal experimentation unethical. He contends that using animals to benefit people amounts to speciesism—arbitrarily valuing humans over animals merely because they are humans. Garner rejects the claim that animal experimentation has been responsible for important medical breakthroughs, pointing out that no one knows whether those innovations could have occurred without the use of animals.

As you read, consider the following questions:
1. According to Garner, how do the most enlightened nations justify animal experimentation?
2. How does the United Kingdom reduce the amount of trivial animal testing, according to the author?
3. In the author's opinion, in what ways do lab animals suffer in addition to experiencing physical pain?

Excerpted from "Animal Rights and Wrongs," by Robert Garner, *Chemistry and Industry*, January 4, 1999. Copyright © 1999 by Chemistry and Industry. Reprinted with permission.

A nimals are exploited by humans in a variety of ways. We eat them, derive clothing and household products from them, use them as a source of entertainment and to improve our psychological well-being, and put them to work for our benefit. Few other issues are as contentious, however, as the use of animals in the laboratory environment.

The Case Against Animal Experimentation

There is a powerful moral case against animal experimentation. If we are asked what gives us the right to exploit animals for our benefit, the answer is usually that we are intellectually superior to other species. A common response is to ask what about those humans—infants and the mentally disabled—whose intellectual capacities may be similar to, or even lower than, at least some animals? If we insist upon treating such humans as superior to animals merely on the grounds that they are human, without any other supporting argument, we are guilty of 'speciesism'. The same argument is used by sexists and racists to justify the dominance of one particular gender or race.

If we reject the idea that humans are superior then, provided we are not prepared to sacrifice some members of our own species to benefit others, we are not permitted to do this to animals either. In other words, if we insist upon granting rights to humans we should also grant them to animals. Animal experimentation then becomes illegitimate, irrespective of the benefits that might result.

No government in the world has accepted the principle that the moral status of animals is on a par with that of humans. Rather, the most enlightened of them—mainly in Western Europe—have recognised that animal suffering matters but, because humans are superior, such suffering should be permitted provided the resulting human benefits are sufficiently important.

The concept of unnecessary suffering is therefore the basis of contemporary animal welfare. In other words, animal experimentation is justified provided any suffering inflicted in the laboratory is perceived to be necessary. This principle would seem to offer no ethical problem for those who anaesthetise animals before carrying out a procedure, and who ensure that they are either killed before regaining consciousness or provided with adequate pain relief. But many procedures—and particularly those concerned with toxicity testing—do involve inflicting suffering on conscious animals. This is unnecessary if alternative methods can be found, if the results are already available, if the research is so badly designed that no meaningful conclusions are likely to result from it, or if it is conducted for trivial reasons.

Reduction and Replacement

To some extent, the regulatory framework in the United Kingdom (UK) does recognise the force of these objections. For instance, the use of alternatives to animal experimentation is encouraged, and recently the government announced an end to the use of animals for testing cosmetics on the grounds that it is trivial and alternative methods exist. Further, Home Office inspectors reviewing project licences are meant to undertake a cost-benefit analysis whereby the proposed suffering to animals is weighed against the benefits likely to accrue from the research.

'Now that you've all had a chance to try the shampoo, we would like you to fill in this questionnaire.'

NAF. © 2001 by *The Spectator*. Reprinted with permission.

In addition to these measures, it is possible to envisage the number of animal experiments being significantly reduced through a much more rigorous application of the principle of unnecessary suffering. The end of cosmetic testing is a step in the right direction, for example, but the number of animals affected is a tiny fraction of the almost three million procedures carried out annually on animals in the UK.

It should also be said that suffering often occurs because of the failure to provide research animals with companionship, mental stimulus or merely adequate space. Too often, this suffering has not been taken seriously in assessments of the justifiability of animal research.

Researchers regularly argue that there is limited scope for alternatives. Given the strides made by science in the post-war world, though, this negativity and conservatism is very odd. Could it just be that using relatively inexpensive, readily available and easily disposable animals has become a habit? Is it not significant, too, that the search for alternatives was speeded up, with considerable success, only when public concern about the use of animals for research began to grow?

It might be thought that the use of animals for medical research is easiest to defend. In fact, the claims made for it are surprisingly shaky. First, although it is true to say that the vast majority of medical innovations have involved the use of animals this proves little because animals have always been routinely used. The key question is whether the same progress would have occurred without the use of animals—a much harder question to answer.

Second, a great deal of modern animal research is concerned with finding remedies for the so-called 'diseases of affluence'—cancer and heart disease—yet these have been shown, primarily by epidemiological studies, to be largely preventable.

Advocating a significant reduction in animal experimentation does not have to be accompanied by an acceptance of the view that animals possess rights. Personally, I do think animals have a higher moral status than society is, at present, willing to give them. At the very least, though, we ought to treat other species with respect, and this means thinking very hard before harming them for our benefit.

"To restrict our acquisition of knowledge by reducing the use of animals in research is not in the best interests of the animals involved."

Animal Experimentation Is Ethical

Henry E. Heffner

Henry E. Heffner is a psychology professor at the University of Toledo. In the following viewpoint, he contends that animal experimentation is ethical because it benefits humans, which in turn benefits lab animals, who depend upon humans for survival. Heffner maintains that the lab environment is safer and healthier than natural habitats, which allows lab animals to reproduce more successfully and continue their genetic lines.

As you read, consider the following questions:
1. According to the author, what is the difference between commensalism and mutualism?
2. Why might a mutualistic relationship develop between humans and wild animals, according to Heffner?
3. What example does Heffner provide as evidence that humans commonly accept arrangements in which the few are sacrificed for the many?

Excerpted from "The Symbiotic Nature of Animal Research," by Henry E. Heffner, *Perspectives in Biology and Medicine*, Autumn 1999. Copyright © 1999 by the Johns Hopkins University Press. Reprinted with permission.

Most animal species commonly used in research had already established relationships with us before they expanded into the laboratory. Laboratory mice and rats are recent descendants of wild house mice (*Mus musculus*) and Norway rats (*Rattus norvegicus*) that evolved as commensals [which obtain food and/or shelter from another at little cost (or benefit) to the host] to live in our houses and feed off our stores of grain. Similarly, dogs are scavengers and are believed to have begun their relationship with us by feeding off our garbage and wastes—as they still do in parts of Africa and the Middle East. Indeed, the coprophagic habits of dogs were well known to polar explorers, who depended on sled dogs, and are still familiar to dog owners with children in diapers. The domestic cat entered into a mutualistic relationship [in which both parties benefit] with us by eating the wild rodents that feed on our grain. Thus, even before becoming domesticated, mice, rats, cats, and dogs were already dependent on humans for their survival.

The Laboratory Niche

During the latter half of the 19th century, it became apparent that the use of animals in research would greatly expand our knowledge of medicine and physiology. This was made apparent by research on animal diseases, such as anthrax and rabies, that helped establish the fact that microorganisms (germs) can cause disease. Indeed, up until that time, the medical community had overwhelmingly rejected the germ theory of disease. It was the application of the animal research of Louis Pasteur and others that led surgeons to begin washing their hands before, instead of after, surgery. At about the same time, animals were used in increasing numbers as physiological research began to expand.

The movement of animals into the laboratory represents their expansion into a new ecological niche. In the case of mice and rats, their relationship with us has been elevated from commensalism to mutualism. Because we now breed them, both their numbers and genetic diversity have increased to the point that there are now well over 200 stocks and strains of laboratory rodents. Indeed, the fact that the various types of laboratory mice and rats are reproductively isolated from each other and have diverged genetically may justify considering them as new species. The fact that humans are responsible for their reproductive isolation is yet another illustration of the well-established principle that one species can affect the evolution of another (compare, for example, the coevolution of flowering plants and the insects that pollinate them).

Some animals, such as cats and dogs, had already established mutualistic relationships with us, and their movement into the laboratory represents an expansion of this relationship. Other animals, such as macaques and chimpanzees, have no close relationship with us outside the laboratory. However, chimpanzees are currently in danger of becoming extinct, and the best chance for their survival may be to establish a mutualistic relationship with us, i.e., to become domesticated. Thus, one obvious survival strategy for chimpanzees would be to expand their use of kin selection [a strategy for perpetuating one's genes] and, capitalizing on their genetic similarity with humans, become essential to medical research, thus increasing their own ability to survive—as well as ours.

Regardless of whether the use of previously domesticated animals in research results in a significant increase in their numbers, they benefit from our research in an indirect, but important way. Domestic animals have developed a dependence on humans no less extreme than the dependence of flowering plants on insects. Because they are now inextricably tied to us, anything that benefits us automatically benefits them and, conversely, anything that threatens our survival is a threat to theirs. For the moment, humans have what appears to be a relatively secure position on this planet. We have achieved this through the use of our intellect, which has allowed us to stabilize our food supply, develop new sources of energy, and hold many diseases at bay (few diseases have actually been eliminated). However, history teaches us that all species eventually become extinct, and the best we can hope for is to delay this inevitability as long as possible. Thus, to restrict our acquisition of knowledge by reducing the use of animals in research is not in the best interests of the animals involved—not only because it decreases a laboratory species' usefulness to us and shuts it out of an ecological niche, but because it reduces the survivability of their major symbiotic partner, us.

Ethical Issues

If research animals benefit from their mutualistic interactions with humans, why would anyone think that these interactions are exploitative and should be discontinued? Although the answers are usually based on personal philosophical principles, there are two points that can be addressed objectively. These are: that life in a laboratory is inferior to that in the wild, and that humans would never accept a similar type of relationship. Both of these points merit scrutiny.

Animals Benefit Too

Humans aren't the only ones to benefit from animal research. Over 80 medicines originally developed for humans are now used to treat pets, farm animals and wildlife. Additionally, skin grafts, organ transplantation techniques, and drug therapies to treat illnesses such as diabetes, heart failure and epilepsy were all developed for animals from their human counterparts.

Americans for Medical Progress, "Benefits of Research," 1999.

The first point is based on the observation that most research animals are not given the opportunity to reproduce, that they are euthanized before they reach senescence, and that they live in environments (laboratories) that differ from their wild habitats. But is the laboratory environment inferior to that found in the wild? As previously noted, animals in the wild suffer high mortality rates, are subject to starvation, predation, and disease, and many, if not most, fail to breed successfully. It would appear that, at worst, the laboratory environment may sometimes be as harsh as life in the wild—for example, when animals are infected in order to study a disease, although even these animals do not have to worry about finding food and shelter or avoiding predators while they are ill. But the fact that animals in captivity live healthier and, in many cases, longer lives than their wild counterparts demonstrates that it is, in fact, a better environment.

Along this line, it should be noted that the natural habitat of animals bred for research is the laboratory—laboratory mice and rats are incapable of surviving in the wild. That they require us to survive does not make them "degenerate" any more than flowering plants that require insects for pollination are degenerate. Thus, animals bred for research are properly viewed as animals that have successfully invaded the laboratory niche, relying heavily on kin selection to perpetuate their genes. Similarly, wild animals brought into the laboratory (or other human environments, such as a zoo) can be viewed as animals exploring a new ecological niche. Interestingly, a mutualistic relationship may develop between humans and wild animals without us directly breeding them. This is because a demand for a wild species may lead to a commercial interest in perpetuating it by maintaining its wild habitat—a classic example being the maintenance of habitats by sportsmen. Thus, we seem to have an inherent tendency to elevate our interactions with other animals to one of mutualism, and our desire to save endangered animals from extinction may be due in part to a desire to hold open the possibility of future mutualistic interactions with them.

Sacrificing the Few for the Many

The second argument against our use of animals is that we would not accept a similar relationship in which some humans would have to suffer in order for others to benefit, and that it is therefore unethical to impose such a relationship on animals. However, we do accept such relationships. While we would like all members of our species to live long and productive lives, we constantly compromise by sacrificing some for the benefit of others—a common example being the altruistic actions of soldiers in time of war. However, a much more common (and largely overlooked) example of sacrifice is our use of the automobile.

In the United States, about 30,000 people are killed each year in accidents involving passenger vehicles. Moreover, automobiles, like animal predators, tend to be inefficient, and over 1.5 million disabling injuries can be attributed to such accidents. Yet no one has had the temerity to seriously propose abolishing the automobile and forcing people to use much safer public transportation (or restricting travel altogether, which would save even more lives). If we accept for ourselves the principle that some must inevitably suffer so that others can enjoy the advantages of private transportation, then should we deny animals the opportunity to make a similar arrangement in order to ensure their very survival?

There is, however, one ethical principle that can be used in evaluating our relationships with animals. It is simply to ask whether we are providing them with a better situation than they would encounter in the wild, i.e., whether we are giving them a "better deal." There are examples of human-animal interactions in which the answer to this question is obviously no—for example, a predator-prey interaction in which animals are hunted to extinction. Domestication, on the other hand, is clearly an interaction in which animals are more successful than they are in the wild. In short, the use of animals by humans, whether it be for the accumulation of knowledge through research or any other reason, typically causes us to work to ensure the continuation of their genetic lines. And that, after all, is the purpose of life.

"Experiments using animals have played a crucial role in the development of modern medical treatments, and they will continue to be necessary."

Animal Research Is Vital to Medicine

Jack H. Botting and Adrian R. Morrison

In the following viewpoint, Jack H. Botting and Adrian R. Morrison claim that all major advances in medicine were discovered through animal experimentation, and they assert that cures for new diseases will also require tests on animals. Botting and Morrison maintain that there is no basic difference between the physiology of animals and humans, which allows scientists to accurately apply information learned from animal experiments to human patients. Jack H. Botting, a retired university lecturer, is the former scientific adviser at the Research Defense Society in London. Adrian R. Morrison is director of the Laboratory for Study of the Brain in Sleep at the University of Pennsylvania School of Veterinary Medicine.

As you read, consider the following questions:
1. According to the authors, what did Louis Pasteur discover from experimenting on animals?
2. How were animals used in the treatment of diabetes, according to Botting and Morrison?
3. How do the authors refute the argument that penicillin would not have been used in patients had it first been administered to guinea pigs?

Experiments using animals have played a crucial role in the development of modern medical treatments, and they will continue to be necessary as researchers seek to alleviate existing ailments and respond to the emergence of new disease. As any medical scientist will readily state, research with animals is but one of several complementary approaches. Some questions, however, can be answered only by animal research. We intend to show exactly where we regard animal research to have been essential in the past and to point to where we think it will be vital in the future. To detail all the progress that relied on animal experimentation would require many times the amount of space allotted to us. Indeed, we cannot think of an area of medical research that does not owe many of its most important advances to animal experiments.

In the mid-19th century, most debilitating diseases resulted from bacterial or viral infections, but at the time, most physicians considered these ailments to be caused by internal derangements of the body. The proof that such diseases did in fact derive from external microorganisms originated with work done by the French chemist Louis Pasteur and his contemporaries, who studied infectious diseases in domestic animals. Because of his knowledge of how contaminants caused wine and beer to spoil, Pasteur became convinced that microorganisms were also responsible for diseases such as chicken cholera and anthrax.

To test his hypothesis, Pasteur examined the contents of the guts of chickens suffering from cholera; he isolated a possible causative microbe and then grew the organism in culture. Samples of the culture given to healthy chickens and rabbits produced cholera, thus proving that Pasteur had correctly identified the offending organism. By chance, he noticed that after a time, cultures of the microorganisms lost their ability to infect. But birds given the ineffective cultures became resistant to fresh batches that were otherwise lethal to untreated birds. Physicians had previously observed that among people who survived a severe attack of certain diseases, recurrence of the disease was rare; Pasteur had found a means of producing this resistance without risk of disease. This experience suggested to him that with the administration of a weakened culture of the disease-causing bacteria, doctors might be able to induce in their patients immunity to infectious diseases.

In similar studies on rabbits and guinea pigs, Pasteur isolated the microbe that causes anthrax and then developed a vaccine against the deadly disease. With the information from animal experiments—obviously of an extent that could never have been carried out on humans—he proved not only that infectious diseases could be produced by microorganisms but also that immunization could protect against these diseases.

Pasteur's findings had a widespread effect. For example, they influenced the views of the prominent British surgeon Joseph Lister, who pioneered the use of carbolic acid to sterilize surgical instruments, sutures and wound dressings, thereby preventing infection of wounds. In 1875 Queen Victoria asked Lister to address the Royal Commission inquiry into vivisection—as the queen put it, "to make some statement in condemnation of these horrible practices." As a Quaker, Lister had spoken publicly against many cruelties of Victorian society, but despite the request of his sovereign, he was unable to condemn vivisection. His testimony to the Royal Commission stated that animal experiments had been essential to his own work on asepsis and that to restrict research with animals would prevent discoveries that would benefit humankind.

Dozens of Vaccines and Antibiotics

Following the work of Pasteur and others, scientists have established causes of and vaccines for dozens of infectious diseases, including diphtheria, tetanus, rabies, whooping cough, tuberculosis, poliomyelitis, measles, mumps and rubella. The investigation of these ailments indisputably relied heavily on animal experimentation: in most cases, researchers identified candidate microorganisms and then administered the microbes to animals to see if they contracted the illness in question.

Similar work continues to this day. Just recently, scientists developed a vaccine against *Hemophilus influenzae* type B (Hib), a major cause of meningitis, which before 1993 resulted in death or severe brain damage in more than 800 children each year in the U.S. Early versions of a vaccine produced only poor, short-lived immunity. But a new vaccine, prepared and tested in rabbits and mice, proved to be powerfully immunogenic and is now in routine use. Within two months of the vaccine's introduction in the U.S. and the U.K., Hib infections fell by 70 percent.

Animal research not only produced new vaccines for the treatment of infectious disease, it also led to the development of antibacterial and antibiotic drugs. In 1935, despite aseptic precautions, trivial wounds could lead to serious infections that resulted in amputation or death. At the same time, in both Europe and the U.S., death from puerperal sepsis (a disease that mothers can contract after childbirth, usually as a result of infection by hemolytic streptococci) occurred in 200 of every 100,000 births. In addition, 60 of every 100,000 men aged 45 to 64 died from lobar pneumonia. When sulfonamide drugs became available, these figures fell dramatically: by 1960 only five out of every 100,000 mothers contracted puerperal sepsis, and only six of every 100,000 middle-aged men succumbed to lobar pneumonia. A range of other infections could also be treated with these drugs.

The story behind the introduction of sulfonamide drugs is instructive. The team investigating these compounds—Gerhard Domagk's group at Bayer Laboratories in Wuppertal-Elberfeld, Germany—insisted that all candidate compounds be screened in infected mice (using the so-called mouse protection test) rather than against bacteria grown on agar plates. Domagk's perspicacity was fortunate: the compound Prontosil, for instance, proved to be extremely potent in mice, but it had no effect on bacteria in vitro—the active antibacterial substance, sulfanilamide, was formed from Prontosil within the body. Scientists synthesized other, even more powerful sulfonamide drugs and used them successfully against many infections. For his work on antibacterial drugs, Domagk won the Nobel Prize in 1939.

A lack of proper animal experimentation unfortunately delayed for a decade the use of the remarkable antibiotic penicillin: Alexander Fleming, working in 1929, did not use mice to examine the efficacy of his cultures containing crude penicillin (although he did show the cultures had no toxic effects on mice and rabbits). In 1940, however, Howard W. Florey, Ernst B. Chain and others at the University of Oxford finally showed penicillin to be dramatically effective as an antibiotic via the mouse protection test.

Despite the success of vaccines and antibacterial therapy, infectious disease remains the greatest threat to human life worldwide. There is no effective vaccine against malaria or AIDS: physicians increasingly face strains of bacteria resistant to current antibacterial drugs; new infectious diseases continue to emerge. It is hard to envisage how new and better vaccines and medicines against infectious disease can be developed without experiments involving animals.

Increased Lifespans

There is not a person in the United States who has not somehow benefited from the results of research involving animals. In the early 1900s, Dr. Simon Brimhall became the first laboratory animal veterinarian. At the time Dr. Brimhall began his work, the average lifespan of adults in the United States was just over 47 years. In the years since, that lifespan has increased almost 60% to 75 years. Almost every advance in medical science that has enabled this longer lifespan has been based on animal research.

American Association for Laboratory Animal Science, "Use of Animals in Biomedical Research: Understanding the Issues."

Research on animals has been vital to numerous other areas in medicine. Open-heart surgery—which saves the lives of an estimated 440,000 people every year in the U.S. alone—is now routine, thanks to 20 years of animal research by scientists such as John Gibbon of Jefferson Medical College in Philadelphia. Replacement heart valves also emerged from years of animal experimentation.

The development of treatments for kidney failure has relied on step-by-step improvement of techniques through animal experiments. Today kidney dialysis and even kidney transplants can save the lives of patients suffering from renal failure as a result of a variety of ailments, including poisoning, severe hemorrhage, hypertension or diabetes. Roughly 200,000 people require dialysis every year in the U.S.; some

11,000 receive a new kidney. Notably, a drug essential for dialysis—heparin—must be extracted from animal tissues and tested for safety on anesthetized animals.

Transplantation of a kidney or any major organ presents a host of complications; animal research has been instrumental in generating solutions to these problems. Experiments on cats helped develop techniques for suturing blood vessels from the host to the donor organ so that the vessels would be strong enough to withstand arterial pressure. Investigators working with rabbits, rodents, dogs and monkeys have also determined ways to suppress the immune system to avoid rejection of the donor organ.

The list continues. Before the introduction of insulin, patients with diabetes typically died from the disease. For more than 50 years, the lifesaving hormone had to be extracted from the pancreas of cattle or pigs; these batches of insulin also had to be tested for safety and efficacy on rabbits or mice.

When we started our scientific careers, the diagnosis of malignant hypertension carried with it a prognosis of death within a year, often preceded by devastating headaches and blindness. Research on anesthetized cats in the 1950s heralded an array of progressively improved antihypertensive medicines, so that today treatment of hypertension is effective and relatively benign. Similarly, gastric ulcers often necessitated surgery with a marked risk of morbidity afterward. Now antiulcer drugs, developed from tests in rats and dogs, can control the condition and may effect a cure if administered with antibiotics to eliminate *Helicobacter pylori* infection.

Common Misconceptions

Much is made in animal-rights propaganda of alleged differences between species in their physiology or responses to drugs that supposedly render animal experiments redundant or misleading. These claims can usually be refuted by proper examination of the literature. For instance, opponents of animal research frequently cite the drug thalidomide as an example of a medicine that was thoroughly tested on animals and showed its teratogenic effect only in humans. But this is not so. Scientists never tested thalidomide in pregnant animals until after fetal deformities were observed in humans.

Once they ran these tests, researchers recognized that the drug did in fact cause fetal abnormalities in rabbits, mice, rats, hamsters and several species of monkey. Similarly, some people have claimed that penicillin would not have been used in patients had it first been administered to guinea pigs, because it is inordinately toxic to this species. Guinea pigs, however, respond to penicillin in exactly the same way as do the many patients who contract antibiotic-induced colitis when placed on long-term penicillin therapy. In both guinea pigs and humans, the cause of the colitis is infection with the bacterium *Clostridium difficile*.

In truth, there are no basic differences between the physiology of laboratory animals and humans. Both control their internal biochemistry by releasing endocrine hormones that are all essentially the same; both humans and laboratory animals send out similar chemical transmitters from nerve cells in the central and peripheral nervous systems, and both react in the same way to infection or tissue injury.

Animal models of disease are unjustly criticized by assertions that they are not identical to the conditions studied in humans. But they are not designed to be so; instead such models provide a means to study a particular procedure. Thus, cystic fibrosis in mice may not exactly mimic the human condition (which varies considerably among patients anyway), but it does provide a way to establish the optimal method of administering gene therapy to cure the disease. Opponents of animal experiments also allege that most illness can be avoided by a change of lifestyle; for example, adoption of a vegan diet that avoids all animal products. Whereas we support the promulgation of healthy practices, we do not consider that our examples could be prevented by such measures.

A Black Hole

Our opponents in this debate claim that even if animal experiments have played a part in the development of medical advances, this does not mean that they were essential. Had such techniques been outlawed, the argument goes, researchers would have been forced to be more creative and thus would have invented superior technologies. Others have suggested that there would not be a gaping black hole in place of animal research but instead more careful and respected clinical and cellular research.

In fact, there was a gaping black hole. No outstanding progress in the treatment of disease occurred until biomedical science was placed on a sound, empirical basis through experiments on animals. Early researchers, such as Pasteur and the 17th-century scientist William Harvey, who studied blood circulation in animals, were not drawn to animal experiments as an easy option. Indeed, they drew on all the techniques available at the time to answer their questions: sometimes dissection of a cadaver, sometimes observations of a patient, sometimes examination of bacteria in culture. At other times, though, they considered experimentation on animals to be necessary.

We would like to suggest an interesting exercise for those who hold the view that animal experiments, because of their irrelevance, have retarded progress: take an example of an advance dependent on animal experiments and detail how an alternative procedure could have provided the same material benefit. A suitable example would be treatment of the cardiac condition known as mitral valve insufficiency, caused by a defect in the heart's mitral valve. The production of prosthetic heart valves stemmed from years of development and testing for efficacy in dogs and calves. The artificial valve can be inserted only into a quiescent heart that has been bypassed by a heart-lung machine—an instrument that itself has been perfected after 20 years' experimentation in dogs. If, despite the benefit of 35 years of hindsight, critics of animal research cannot present a convincing scenario to show how effective treatment of mitral valve insufficiency could have developed any other way, their credibility is suspect.

Will animal experiments continue to be necessary to resolve extant medical problems? Transgenic animals with a single mutant gene have already provided a wealth of new information on the functions of proteins and their roles in disease; no doubt they will continue to do so. We also anticipate major progress in the treatment of traumatic injury to the central nervous system. The dogma that it is impossible to restore function to damaged nerve cells in the mammalian spinal cord has to be reassessed in the light of recent animal research indicating that nerve regeneration is indeed possible. It is only a matter of time before treatments begin to work. We find it difficult to envision how progress in this field—and so many others in biological and medical science—can be achieved in the future without animal experiments.

> "*What we found, in our search for the source of continued animal experimentation, was not 'science,' but mass confusion kept in spin by mass deception.*"

Animal Experimentation Is Unscientific

C. Ray Greek and Jean Swingle Greek

C. Ray Greek and Jean Swingle Greek argue in the following viewpoint that animal experimentation is unscientific because it erroneously assumes that animals and humans are similar at the cellular and molecular level. In fact, the authors contend that human and animal physiology are so different that many of the drugs and treatments that are approved after animal testing turn out to harm and even kill thousands of people each year. Moreover, the authors contend that animal testing has not been responsible for major breakthroughs in medical science. C. Ray Greek is an anesthesiologist and Jean Swingle Greek is a veterinarian.

As you read, consider the following questions:
1. What difference between dogs and humans makes dogs unsuitable as test subjects for surgery on the aorta, according to the authors?
2. According to the authors, how many people are killed by legal drugs each year?
3. What is "scaling," according to the authors?

Excerpted from *Sacred Cows and Golden Geese: The Human Cost of Experiments on Animals*, by C. Ray Greek and Jean Swingle Greek (New York, NY: The Continuum International Publishing Group, Inc., 2000). Copyright © 2000 by C. Ray Greek, MD, and Jean Swingle Greek, DVM. Reprinted by permission of The Continuum International Publishing Group, Inc.

C omparative medicine may not be everyone's idea of a riv-
eting dinner topic, but it is ours. [Our book *Sacred Cows
and Golden Geese: The Human Cost of Experiments on Animals*]
grew out of our meal-time conversations during the 1980s.
Those were the years of our professional education . . . one of
us as a veterinarian, and the other as an anesthesiologist.

A Sacred Cow

When our animal and human patients exhibited the same
symptoms, discussion became most heated. This was because diagnoses and treatment plans for animals frequently
differed for humans. Pitting the veterinarian's dictates on the
one hand against the physician's on the other, we would each
get huffy and self-righteous, then whip out our textbooks to
prove our accuracy. Many references later, sure enough, according to the books, we were both right.

Well, this was puzzling! These discrepancies flew in the
face of what we had been taught to revere. Animal experimentation was an inviolable convention—a political *sacred
cow*. Everything we had been taught, from fetal pigs forward,
suggested that animals were just like humans, a bit furry and
funny looking perhaps, but otherwise just the same.

Like everyone, we had been convinced by many familiar
determinants: animal experimentation for human medical
research had a time-honored history. Milestones supposedly
garnered from animal studies were constantly in the media.
As medical students, we were well familiar with the government's requirement for animal assays in drug development
and its financial rewards to research institutions. Certainly,
grant money for such projects was vital to the incomes of our
teachers and universities. Indeed, our medical training piv-
oted on assumed anatomic, biochemical, and physiological
characteristics shared by man and beast.

This sizable and persuasive rationalism averred that animals were ideal test beds for human therapies. So, why then
was Ray's human patient with high cholesterol developing
coronary heart disease and Jean's dog with high cholesterol
experiencing a thyroid disorder? Why do women who have
had hysterectomies need to fight osteoporosis while neutered
cats live longer, healthier lives? And why are humans not

vaccinated for parvo and dogs for rubella? Our dinner conversations suggested that most animal diseases simply do not occur in humans. Conversely, the major killers of humankind are extraordinarily rare among the four-legged set.

Isomorphism

Plainly, if there was parity, it was not universal. Sure, the basics are the same. Fundamental cell activity and metabolic processes—the stuff of research decades ago—correspond in animals and humans. Still, we thought, why did scientists use animals back when human autopsy, tissue culture techniques, or human observation could have provided the same information? Some animal experimentation led to developments. But in how many cases were the animals *necessary?* Animals can be used to grow viruses, but so can petri dishes and human tissue cultures. All mammalian blood—animal and human—has components in common, so why not use human blood for totally accurate results? Moreover, when it came to present-day research—mostly involving microbiology on the most complex levels—why scrutinize species whose physiologic response to disease, disease manifestation, and disease incidence so clearly deviates from human response? Logic, it seemed to us, even back then when we had but few comparisons, was somehow amiss.

Both of us had performed animal experimentation. We knew from experience how similar the gross anatomy of animals and humans is, and how dissimilar are the details. For example, all mammals have a four-chambered heart that pumps blood, but our own education taught that at the cellular level mammals react very differently to medications. All land mammals have four limbs, but attempts to test surgeries of the aorta on dogs fail because dogs' circulation is different in part due to their walking on four extremities while we walk on two. Animals and humans both secrete gastric juices and other chemicals. However, the gastric fluid in dogs' stomachs is much more acidic than ours. This is why Fido can gobble down uncouth matter without upsetting his stomach, and humans cannot.

Scientists have a name for one-to-one correspondence between all elements in two or more living systems. *Isomorph-*

ism. Clearly, animals are not isomorphic with humans. With systems as complex as the human body, very small dissimilarities not only negate isomorphism but also have radical implications. Grossly, animals are alike, that is why we are all part of the animal kingdom. We differ on the cellular and molecular level, and, importantly, *that is where disease occurs.*

We, the tireless medical students, became more inquisitive. We asked the kind of questions everyone asks when confronted with the subject of animal experimentation. No one really wants to torture animals, but look where a history of animal experimentation has led us. Where would we be today without the antibiotics, the scanners, the modern surgical techniques, and the host of medications used daily to treat everything from heart disease to arthritis to cancer? If animal models are not employed, what or who will be? Few people aspire to be the first patient of an inexperienced surgeon or the first person to take a new drug. Moreover, we rationalized, is it not reassuring to know that new advances have been thoroughly tested on animals, found not only safe, but also effective?

How Safe and Effective?

But how safe, how effective are these animal-modeled advances? Investigating further, we learned that though cardiac-bypass surgery was practiced extensively on animals, when first tried on humans, the patients actually died. Penicillin kills guinea pigs and is not effective in rabbits. Were these troubling examples common ones? Or were they exceptions to the rule? Apparently not, we found. Roughly fifteen percent of all hospital admissions are caused by adverse medication reactions. And legal drugs, which made their way to the public via animals, kill approximately 100,000 people per year. That is more than all illegal drugs combined and costs the general public over $136 billion in health care expenses.

We found the actual merit of using animal tissues—in the culture medium, as heart valves or for insulin, or to produce monoclonal antibodies, and so forth—was by no means as advantageous as we had been led to believe. There were heavy risks, sometimes resulting in human illness and even death. And no one was mentioning the less dangerous treatments these therapies delayed. Likewise underestimated was the potential for animal-borne viruses that might mutate into a more deadly and contagious form in the human body. When we began to collect data, the fatally infectious protein particles called *prions* (which could inhabit all animal tissue and which medicine has no way to thwart) had yet to reveal themselves. Now that prions have been front page news, from the incidences of Mad Cow disease, everyone should know that mining animals for treatments is courting disaster.[1] But they do not.

We had been led to believe that the majority of medical advances had come about as the result of research carried out on animals. Now we wondered was this truth or propaganda?

We do not deny that we are both "animal lovers," to some extent motivated by our affection for animals and our concern for their well being. However, more essentially, we are both medical doctors and scientists. For ten years, Ray performed the most demanding branch of anesthesiology in cardiopulmonary and transplantation surgeries. Jean became one of the top veterinary dermatologists in the world. We have both published extensively in the scientific literature. Our lifestyle and careers are grounded in science. Logic, reason, data, causal relationships, verifiability, repeatability, and all other tenets of the scientific paradigm—these provide the hard scientific foundation for our choices, both personal and professional.

Misleading, Unnecessary, and Dangerous

We were finding, through scientific research, that extrapolating data from animals to humans is either *misleading, unnecessary, dangerous,* or all three.

The strongest tenet that arises from science is predictability. To be reliable, a model should have predictive value. That is science. In medicine, strong models assume four factors: the same symptoms, the same postulated origin of disease, the same neurobiological mechanism, and the same treatment response. The truth is that though certain

---

1. Studies completed in 1999 suggest that a particular strain of prions that causes bovine spongiform encephalopathy—or mad cow disease—is also responsible for causing a new variant of human Creutzfeldt–Jakob disease. Both diseases are fatal.

animals may fulfill some of the same criteria as humans in some incidences, no animal consistently fulfills all four. This means that animals are not strong models for human disease.

It also means that all data recovered from animal-model experiments must be *scaled*. Scaling is a scientific term that, generally, refers to "the fudge factor." Since we are all putting our lives and the lives of our loved ones in the hands of supposedly rigorous science, is not a model that requires so much fudging grossly inadequate—especially since humans themselves provide the perfect model?

Mortality and Animal Experiments

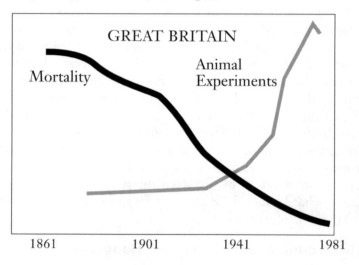

American Anti-Vivisection Society, "Health and Humane Research: Helping People and Animals," 1994.

Given all these peculiarities, we began to ponder just how humans do benefit from animal experimentation. We asked physicians how it had specifically contributed to their field. Surgeons denied knowledge of any specific contributions, but referred us to pediatricians. Pediatricians knew of no significant achievements in pediatrics that relied on animals, but referred us to psychiatrists. Psychiatrists pointed out the drawbacks to studying psychosis in mice and suggested we contact the internists. And it continued. Each specialist, though unaware of true animal-model successes in his own field, was convinced that other specialists were reliant on this protocol. They too had bought what was fast appearing to us as a bill of goods.

Delving deeper through the scientific literature, searching for the substantive development history of explicit drugs, technologies, and techniques, we found a broad gap between prevailing thought and actual incident. Commonly attributed to animal experimentation, the development of drugs and technologies did *not* rely on animals. We began to collect data on these disparities. Of course, we were not the first to question the relevance of animal experimentation. And as we researched we uncovered to what extent it had been criticized.

Doubters

Among our predecessors we found many men and women who had dared to refute the animal model. They expressed doubts on the order of these from Dr. M. Beddow Bayly, who in 1961 wrote:

> The paramount need for a clear and documented account of past achievements arises from the prevalent custom of those medical authorities who set out to support and defend the practice of experimenting on living animals so far to distort historical facts as to create the impression in the mind of the public that every single medical diagnosis and treatment had depended for its discovery and application on vivisection. . . . Happily, even the briefest perusal of the available evidence shows falsity of these claims and provides historical proof of the supreme value of clinical observation and experiment when contrasted with the doubtful and often misleading practice of animal experimentation.

In other words, Dr. Bayly felt as we had begun to feel—that most advances were due to clinical observations by doctors and nurses on their human patients.

So there we were, with our growing pile of data. It reflected how many ways and for how many years, we had all been duped. Agreeing with the Dr. Baylys of the world and troubled by the utter lack of scientific grounding in animal experimentation, we wanted to know why it persisted. Perhaps we had missed something? We decided to go to the animal experimenters themselves and ask why and how animal experiments were important.

The animal experimentation lobby has very persuasive arguments. Time after time we thought, "Surely this is an advance that must be credited to the animal model." However, once we actually looked up the true origins of the advance in the scientific literature, we either found a clinical discovery, serendipity, or some other non-animal based discovery had previously revealed the knowledge, which animal experimenters later "validated" in animals. Animal experimentation lobbyists or public-relations people did not, of course, mention these preemptive revelations.

Follow the Money

The incidences where actual medical history deviated from that presented by pro-animal experimenters grew and grew. They are what *Sacred Cows and Golden Geese* is about—in part. Our other subject, and indeed underlying theme, is why animal experimentation continues.

Anyone who asks "why" has only to follow the money to find an answer. Like the goose who laid the golden egg, animal experimentation is a source of infinite financing. Tracing the funding dollars, we found a medical-research system corrupted by lobbying groups, opportunistic scientists, irresponsible drug companies, unlearned public officials, and clogged bureaucracies, all profiting off the animal model's golden eggs.

Science is a lot of things, but fundamentally, it is not public relations. It is not bureaucracy. It is not trends. It is not professional societies, nor special-interest groups. It is not a commodity. Though public relations, trends, organizations, bureaucrats, and money may drive it, science is not any of these. However, science is shaped by our perceptions, just as our experience of the sun is affected by the earth's atmosphere. The dollars go where the concern rests.

What we found, in our search for the source of continued animal experimentation, was not "science," but mass confusion kept in spin by mass deception. The general public has more confidence in hype than in facts, possibly because the facts, being largely in scientific journals, are mostly unavailable and inscrutable.

The other reason that animal experimentation continues is simply the momentum of convention. It is a bit like Newton's first law of motion—objects in motion tend to remain that way. Animal experiments continue because they have occurred for a long time.

Periodical Bibliography

The following articles have been selected to supplement the diverse views presented in this chapter. Addresses are provided for periodicals not indexed in the *Readers' Guide to Periodical Literature*, the *Alternative Press Index*, the *Social Sciences Index*, or the *Index to Legal Periodicals and Books*.

Carol J. Adams	"Whose Science Is It Anyway? A Feminist Exploration," *AV Magazine*, Winter 1998.
Americans for Medical Progress	"Helping the Public Understand Animal Research in Medicine," http://amprogress.org/faq.htm.
Carolee McGill Barker	"My Personal Views on Animal Experimentation," www.geocities.com/pmainfo/anres.html.
Neal D. Barnard and Stephen R. Kaufman	"Animal Research Is Wasteful and Misleading," *Scientific American*, February 1, 1997.
Susan Brink	"Clashing Passions," *U.S. News & World Report*, May 4, 1998.
Michael E. DeBakey	"Hype and Hypocrisy on Animal Rights," *Wall Street Journal*, December 12, 1996.
Foundation for Biomedical Research	"Position Paper on Animal Research," 1997, www.fbre.search.org/position_paper.html.
Sandra Larson	"A Former Experimenter Reflects," New England Anti-Vivisection Society website, www.neavs.org/articles.larson.html.
Andrew N. Rowan	"The Benefits and Ethics of Animal Research," *Scientific American*, February 1997.
Josette Shiner and Bonnie Erbe	"A Place for PETA at the Science Table?" *Washington Times*, February 1, 1997.
Erik Stokstad	"Humane Science Finds Sharper and Kinder Tools," *Science*, November 5, 1999.
Peter Tatchell	"Animal Tests Kept Protease Inhibitors off the Market," *Knight-Ridder/Tribune News Service*, August 12, 1997.
Wendeline L. Wagner	"They Shoot Monkeys, Don't They?" *Harper's Magazine*, August 1997.

CHAPTER 3

How Should Animal Experimentation Be Conducted?

Chapter Preface

While most people know that mice are used in research laboratories, many would be surprised to learn that farm animals—such as cows, pigs, and chickens—are also experimented on. Like mice, some farm animals are used to study human diseases, but most are used in agricultural research.

Farm animals used in biomedical research are used as models in the study of human health problems. For example, researchers at the University of California, San Diego use chickens to study the effects of nicotine on prenatal organisms. In agricultural research, animals are used to develop more cost-effective methods of raising them for food. For example, chickens are used to find ways to increase egg production and increase the size of broiler chickens. A researcher at the University of Georgia developed a device that when inserted into the nasal cartilage of male chickens prevents them from sticking their heads into the cages of laying hens and eating their food.

Currently, the Animal Welfare Act (AWA)—which governs the way that laboratory animals are treated—protects most animals used in biomedical research but does not cover those used in agricultural research. Many critics of animal experimentation argue that all farm animals should be brought under the protection of the AWA because farm animals feel pain in the same way that other animals covered by the act do. On the other hand, advocates of animal experimentation contend that including all farm animals in the AWA would make agricultural research more expensive and might in turn raise food prices. In addition, they point out that while many object to the use of dogs and primates in research, most people are less concerned about the welfare of animals they commonly consume for food.

Since its enactment in 1966, the Animal Welfare Act has been amended many times to change the way that scientists conduct experiments on animals. The authors in the following chapter debate how animal experimentation should be conducted. Even if farm animals used in agricultural research are eventually covered under the AWA, the debate about the welfare of lab animals will continue.

"Self-regulation ensures that research institutions go virtually unchecked in terms of animal welfare."

The Animal Research Industry Needs More Oversight

In Defense of Animals

In Defense of Animals works to end the institutional exploitation of animals. In the following viewpoint, the organization contends that government agencies charged with enforcing laws protecting the welfare of laboratory animals are ineffective. The organization argues that agencies such as the Institutional Animal Care and Use Committees don't protect animals because their members are predominantly researchers who approve each other's work. As a result of lax oversight, many laboratory animals suffer needless pain during unnecessary experiments.

As you read, consider the following questions:
1. How many formal complaints did the U.S. Department of Agriculture file under the Animal Welfare Act between 1992 and April 1998, according to the organization?
2. According to In Defense of Animals, what five duties are the Institutional Animal Care and Use Committees charged with?
3. According to the organization, for what infractions has the U.S. Department of Agriculture cited the University of California at San Francisco?

In the U.S. there are over 1200 facilities registered with the U.S. Department of Agriculture [USDA] as "active" in the conduct of animal research. While many of these facilities are privately funded pharmaceutical and biotechnology firms, many more are universities and other institutions that are the beneficiaries of public funding. The lion's share of public funding for medical research in this country is provided by the National Institutes of Health (NIH).

More than a decade ago, the famed investigative journalist Jack Anderson wrote, "the NIH gives away more than $5 billion a year on research. Whether that money is well spent is anybody's guess. For the most part, NIH blindly trusts that the money went for credible research." Subsequent Congressional hearings on scientific fraud and misconduct laid bare the woeful lack of oversight provided to research by NIH.

Today, while the NIH's budget has literally quadrupled, improved mechanisms for oversight have not been implemented. The victims of this lax system for research are many: the taxpayers who fund research of questionable validity and value; the patients who are involved in clinical studies; and the animals, an estimated 18.5 million of whom are used annually in biomedical experiments.

What follows is a brief overview of the laws, regulations and institutional structures regulating the conduct of research on animals.

Animal Welfare Act

In 1966, "Concentration Camps for Dogs," a *Life Magazine* exposé on the conditions at dog dealer kennels, sparked public outrage and led to the passage of the federal Animal Welfare Act. The Animal Welfare Act (AWA) sets forth minimum standards of care for animals used in research and other forms of commerce. These standards relate to specifics such as sanitation, housing, ventilation, transportation and the provision of adequate veterinary care. With regard to research, the AWA specifies that pain and distress must be minimized in experimental procedures.

It further specifies that alternatives to the use of animals be considered by the principal investigator. It does not, however, restrict any procedures or conditions to which an animal can be subject during the course of an experiment.

And while the AWA states that no animal can be used in more than one major operative experiment with recovery, it allows exceptions that render this provision essentially meaningless.

The AWA does not govern the care and use of rodents, birds and farm animals, because those species were specifically exempted from regulations promulgated under the AWA by the U.S. Department of Agriculture (USDA). Unfortunately, these species represent approximately 80 percent of all animals used in research.

In October 2000, the USDA agreed to include mice, rats and birds under the AWA in response to a legal petition submitted by animal advocates. Later that month, however, Senator Thad Cochran (R-MS) successfully included a provision in the Agriculture appropriations bill that blocked funding for USDA's efforts to write regulations to include these species under the AWA. Thus the status of these animals, deemed "non-animals" by government bureaucracy, remains in limbo.

The USDA's Animal and Plant Health Inspection Service/Animal Care division is responsible for enforcing the AWA. It does so by conducting routine unannounced inspections and by initiating investigations into continuing non-compliance with the AWA.

The USDA has been routinely found by its own Inspector General (IG) to have failed to adequately enforce the AWA. In three audits issued in 1992, 1994 and 1996, the IG found the USDA's Animal and Plant Health Inspection Service fails to make inspections with reliable frequency, lets violations go uncorrected for too long and imposes penalties only if violators agree to pay. The penalties are so low, the 1994 audit states, that licensees consider them "part of the cost of doing business."

Chronic understaffing has played a role in the USDA's poor performance, but so too has a bureaucratic coziness with the industries that the agency is supposed to regulate. The USDA has historically been reluctant to challenge research institutions, and has pursued only the most egregious and highly publicized violations by research facilities. For example, In Defense of Animals [an organization that works to improve the welfare of animals] estimates that between 1992 through March 2001, the USDA filed 417 formal complaints under the AWA. Of those 417, only 21 were filed against registered research facilities. Most of those complaints were settled with little more than slaps on the wrist when offending facilities agreed to pay a fine and promise to cease and desist violating the Animal Welfare Act. Unfortunately, even when the USDA does take action, its authority to stop violations of the Act is limited. Unlike with dog dealers, the USDA has no authority to revoke the licenses of research facilities that do not comply with federal animal welfare laws. This loophole in the Act allows facilities like The Coulston Foundation, a New Mexico primate-testing laboratory that has been formally charged an unprecedented *four times* by the USDA for AWA violations (most involving negligent chimpanzee deaths), to continue to operate.

Public Health Service Policy for the Care and Use of Laboratory Animals

The Public Health Service (PHS) Policy on Humane Care and Use of Laboratory Animals sets forth the requirements for all research, training, testing, and related activities involving animals that are supported or conducted by agencies of the PHS, including the National Institutes of Health (NIH). The Office of Laboratory Animal Welfare (OLAW) is responsible for enforcing this policy at the NIH. By law this agency is required to disqualify any institution that chronically violates PHS policy from receipt of PHS funds. In practice, the agency relies on a meaningless policy of "institutional self-regulation," and has a well-documented history of inactivity and whitewashing of allegations of noncompliance against research institutions.

OLAW was formerly known as the Office of Protection from Research Risks (OPRR). In addition to animal research oversight, OPRR was also responsible for overseeing human based research, relying on a similar policy of institutional self-regulation to do so. In 1999, an expert panel found protections for human research subjects to be inadequate and oversight of human-based research to be entirely lacking. As a result, responsibility for oversight of human based research was moved away from the NIH (which was deemed to have a conflict of interest in providing such oversight) and placed under the auspices of a newly created office in the Department of Health and Human Services. The agency's oversight of animal research, although similarly plagued with conflicts and laxities, was not examined. Responsibility for this important activity remained with the NIH and its newly renamed OLAW office.

Institutional Animal Care and Use Committees

Amendments to the Animal Welfare Act, passed in 1985, mandated the establishment of Institutional Animal Care and Use Committees, or IACUC's, at all federally funded research institutions utilizing animals.

By law, IACUC's are supposed to: 1) review animal research protocols to determine if the appropriate animal model and appropriate numbers of animals have been chosen, and if personnel are properly trained and knowledgeable in the proper use of anesthesia, analgesia and euthanasia, 2) ensure that no alternatives to using animals are available, 3) ensure that all animal care and use at the facility is in compliance with the Animal Welfare Act and PHS Policy on the Care and Use of Laboratory Animals (if PHS funds are involved), 4) conduct semi-annual, unannounced inspections of facilities to ensure the humane care, treatment and transport of animals, and 5) support the attending veterinarian, making sure he or she has access to all animal facilities, and aiding the veterinarian in training of personnel and review of protocols and facilities.

Members of the IACUC are predominantly scientists who use animals and veterinarians who work with them. By law, each IACUC must include one "non-affiliated" member who is supposed to represent the concerns of the community.

On paper, IACUC's are the lynchpin of animal welfare enforcement. In practice, however, IACUC's are little more than rubberstamps, with researchers approving each other's protocols. The public member is frequently chosen for his or her willingness to go along. Those who do raise questions and object to experimental procedures are outnumbered; several have been harassed and intimidated off the committees.

A study published in *Science* magazine on July 27, 2001

confirmed the low reliability of IACUC reviews of animal experiments. Funded by the National Science Foundation, the three-year study found that approval decisions made by university animal use committees in the United States are unreliable when it comes to experimental procedures involving animals.

Slack Enforcement

The Animal and Plant Health Inspection Service (APHIS), under the direction of the U.S. Department of Agriculture (USDA), is supposed to inspect animal dealers and research facilities, and enforce the Animal Welfare Act (AWA). In 1992 and 1995, APHIS was itself inspected by the Office of the Inspector General (OIG), which issued scathing reports documenting APHIS's inability to accomplish this task. Two particularly relevant passages include: ". . . APHIS cannot ensure humane care and treatment at all facilities covered by the Animal Welfare Act," and "APHIS does not have the authority, under current legislation, to effectively enforce the requirements of the Animal Welfare Act."

American Anti-Vivisection Society, *Answers to Typical Questions About Animal Experimentation*, 1996.

Privately, conscientious members of IACUC's have confided about the pressures they face from investigators expecting total academic freedom, and from administrations wanting to bring in grant dollars. This pressure leads to approval of protocols with little scientific merit as well as those with questionable animal use. At New York University [NYU], the IACUC approved Ron Wood's crack-smoking experiments even though, in the words of one IACUC member, everything Wood was studying on monkeys had already been well documented in humans. The IACUC also approved a protocol allowing water deprivation of monkeys for 18 hours/day. The approval was made over the objections of several members and under stiff pressure from the administration. (Wood's annual grant of $500,000 brought in excess of $300,000 annually to NYU for "overhead" administrative costs.)

The NIH relies explicitly on IACUC's to ensure compliance with federal animal welfare laws and policies. However, when IACUC's have been documented to be failing to uphold their legally mandated duties, the NIH has taken no action. For example, since 1998, the USDA has cited the University of California at San Francisco [UCSF] repeatedly for oversight failings. According to inspection reports, the UCSF IACUC has failed, among other things, to ensure that l) alternatives to animals are adequately explored; 2) pain and distress are minimized through the appropriate use of anesthesia and analgesia; 3) researchers adhere to approved procedures; and 4) all personnel working with animals are adequately trained and qualified. Yet, the NIH has taken no action against this institution; its federal research funding, totaling over $290 million annually, continues uninterrupted. Between 1995 and 2000, the IACUC at The Coulston Foundation was found by the USDA and by the Association for Assessment and Accreditation of Laboratory Animal Care International to be even worse. Yet the NIH only belatedly disqualified the lab from receipt of federal research funds in June 2001, years after the foundation was first documented to be violating animal welfare laws. Prior to June 2001, the NIH had given the foundation in excess of $20 million, including $3.1 million in "supplemental awards" granted solely as a public bailout of this failing private corporation. During that time period, the foundation's IACUC was basically non-functioning and the lab continually violated the Animal Welfare Act.

Conclusion

Although research institutions are quick to claim that they adhere to numerous federal laws protecting animals in laboratories, in reality, oversight of animal research is minimal. A policy of institutional self-regulation ensures that research institutions go virtually unchecked in terms of animal welfare violations. The only exception to this rule has been when whistleblowers have courageously come forward to expose wrongdoing. In many cases, however, animal welfare whistleblowers have suffered severe retaliation for their actions. Unfortunately, although Congress stressed the importance of whistleblowers in upholding laws to protect laboratory animals, the Animal Welfare Act offers only weak and unenforceable protections for individuals who expose wrongdoing.

> "[Researchers are required] to provide
> evidence that the proposed research . . .
> couldn't be carried out in a scientifically
> valid way without using live animals."

Animal Experimentation Is Sufficiently Regulated

Delmas Luedke

In the following viewpoint, Delmas Luedke argues that sufficient oversight guarantees the welfare of laboratory animals. He claims that Institutional Animal Care and Use Committees—which are charged by the U.S. Department of Agriculture to oversee research projects using animals—make sure that proposed animal research is not redundant. The committees also monitor the use, care, and handling of all laboratory animals, he contends. The Reverend Delmas Luedke is manager for Spiritual Care at Swedish Medical Center in Seattle and has been a member of an Institutional Animal Care and Use Committee.

As you read, consider the following questions:
1. According to Luedke, what are some of the benefits that have accrued as a result of animal testing?
2. What are the concerns of those opposed to animal testing, according to the author?
3. How often do Institutional Animal Care and Use Committees review each research protocol, according to the author?

Using animals for biomedical research evokes strong emotions among those on both sides of the issue.

People who favor the use of animals in research cite the many benefits that have accrued to us as individuals and as a society. Among the gains are many antibiotics, vaccines, erythropoietin for the treatment of renal failure and certain anemias, the development of chemotherapies that have become standard treatment for combating or in some cases eradicating cancer and many of the procedures that have paved the way for organ transplants in human beings. The research also has improved the health and quality of life for animals.

On the other hand, those who oppose the use of any animals for research are concerned that such animals are exposed to too much suffering and that there are better alternatives than animal research.

It is unfortunate that the debate gets cast in such a way that it implies that one group cares about animals and another group does not. It is not an issue of caring or not caring. Rather, the issue is how to reduce total suffering for humans and animals. There is strong evidence that without animal research and the modern medicines stemming from that research, overall suffering from disease in this world would be greater, not less.

Oversight

However, animals should not be exploited or abused in the process of research. To address that valid concern, research facilities are now required to have an Institutional Animal Care and Use Committee to oversee animal research. The IACUC is made up of research experts, licensed veterinarians and members of the community at large.

I have been a member of such a committee at a local research institution. We monitored each research protocol regarding the use, care and handling of animals. The researcher had to provide evidence that the proposed research had not already been done and that the proposed protocol couldn't be carried out in a scientifically valid way without using live animals.

These committees limit the number of animals used to a minimum required to reasonably test the hypothesis of the study. If an animal is dying, veterinarians determine when euthanasia is indicated in order to minimize suffering. The IACUC reviews each research protocol in detail every six months, in addition to the continuous monitoring done by veterinarians.

Minimizing Total Suffering

In a world without disease or suffering, research using animals (or humans) would not be necessary. But until that day, such research allows scientists to systematically study the diseases that plague us.

Use of Laboratory Animals

Species	Numbers Used in 1997	Numbers Used in 1996	Numbers Used in 1995
Guinea pigs	272,797	299,011	333,374
Rabbits	309,322	338,574	354,076
Hamsters	217,079	246,415	248,402
Dogs	75,429	82,454	89,420
Primates	56,381	52,327	50,206
Cats	26,091	26,035	29,569
Farm animals[*]	159,742	154,344	163,985
Other animals[*]	150,987	146,579	126,426
TOTAL	1,267,828	1,345,739	1,395,463

[*] Some birds, fish, frogs and some rats and mice are included in the category of "other animals."

Lynn Johnson Langer, *Medical and Healthcare Marketplace Guide*, 1999.

Using animals in carefully controlled and monitored studies not only can achieve this goal, but also minimizes total suffering. Many potential drugs never reach human testing because they are found to be toxic in animal tests. Animal research also is not just about humans using animals for the benefit of humans. If animal testing confirms the potential benefits and safety of a drug or procedure, then the research moves into the realm of testing on humans. The big difference, of course, is that the consent of the individual is required in the case of human subjects.

It is true that the consent of the animal for participation cannot be obtained. But that is true for most human-animal relationships. The issue may not be so much consent as of respect. From our sacred writings we are taught that all life is sacred. Therefore, all life is to be respected and honored. When a family pauses to pray before eating, they are in essence respecting the source from which came the food, and if the meal contains meat, respecting the life of the animal that made the meal possible.

Some contend that it is morally superior for humans to consume only plants and the products of living animals, such as milk; however, it remains morally acceptable in our society to consume meat for food. If it is acceptable to consume meat for food, it is morally acceptable to utilize animals for research for the purpose of alleviating greater suffering.

The real value of animal research is seen in the lives of people who directly benefit from this research. I have been fortunate to experience with the parents of an 18-month-old child the joy and relief at seeing her go from certain death to having the opportunity to develop her life as a healthy, productive adult because of a bone marrow transplant. I've shared the gratitude of a young parent who is no longer confined to the demands of a dialysis machine three times a week. As a result of a kidney transplant, she can now care and provide for her family. That has been a sacred experience.

Beyond the personal satisfactions that I have experienced in my ministry, we as a society are enriched because of the new life and improved quality of the lives of people benefiting from animal research.

Animals used for research purposes ought never be treated with disregard, nor should they be used frivolously. We must continue to honor all life and continue to use our best judgments and scientific techniques in minimizing the suffering of those animals (and humans) that make it possible, through appropriate research, to combat the medical problems that confront us.

> "*Nonhuman primate research has led to major medical breakthroughs in the treatment and prevention of diseases such as polio, Rh disease, and hepatitis.*"

Experimenting on Nonhuman Primates Is Vital to Science

Southwest Foundation for Biomedical Research

The Southwest Foundation for Biomedical Research is one of eight federally funded Regional Primate Research Centers that conduct biomedical research using primates. In the following viewpoint, the foundation argues that because monkeys and apes are so physically similar to humans, they make excellent models for studying infectious and chronic human diseases. In fact, the foundation contends that research involving non-human primates has led to major medical breakthroughs in the treatment and prevention of human diseases that would not have been possible without the use of non-human primates.

As you read, consider the following questions:
1. Of the 1.35 million animals used in medical research in 1996, what percentage were primates, according to the foundation?
2. According to the foundation, why are non-human primates used in studying menopause?
3. What percentage of research animals do not experience pain related to experimental use, according to the foundation?

Excerpted from "Primates in Biomedical Research," by Southwest Foundation for Biomedical Research, www.primate.wisc.edu/pin/research/p39-41.html, 1999. Copyright © 1999 by the Southwest Foundation for Biomedical Research. Reprinted with permission.

Background on Animal Research

During the 20th century, virtually every major advance in medical knowledge and treatment involved research using animal models. Two-thirds of Nobel Prizes in Medicine awarded since 1901 were won for discoveries that required the use of animals.

Research involving animals is vital to continued medical progress in both human medicine and veterinary medicine. Animal research has saved lives, extended life expectancy, and improved the quality of human life by enabling scientists to conduct critical experiments that identified ways to prevent, treat, and cure diseases.

There has been a steady decline in the numbers of animals used in medical research as documented by the U.S. Department of Agriculture (USDA), and medical research with human subjects is more common than animal-based biomedical research.

About 1.35 million animals were used in medical research in 1996 according to the USDA. Approximately 90 percent of the animals used in research are rats, mice, and other rodents specifically bred for research. One percent are cats and dogs, and less than 0.5 percent are primates. Many other types of animals also are used in research, including pigs, sheep, cows, rabbits, and fish.

While the percentage of research efforts involving nonhuman primates is small, nonhuman primate research has led to major medical breakthroughs in the treatment and prevention of diseases such as polio, Rh disease, and hepatitis.

Regional Primate Research Centers: A National Scientific Resource

The National Institutes of Health (NIH) Regional Primate Research Centers (RPRCs) are a unique network of nonhuman primate research laboratories established as a scientific resource of regional and national importance to the advancement of biomedical and behavioral research.

They provide for the development and study of nonhuman primate models that are essential for basic and clinical research on human health and disease-related processes. Research at the primate centers also focuses on characterizing diseases that naturally occur in nonhuman primates, some of which pose threats to human health.

The RPRCs centralize facilities and scientific expertise in primate research, providing a cost-effective mechanism to address national needs for medical and behavioral research relying on a broad range of nonhuman primate species.

There currently are eight Regional Primate Research Centers distributed around the country. Seven were established in the early 1960s in Washington, Oregon, Georgia, Massachusetts, Wisconsin, Louisiana, and California. The eighth Regional Primate Research Center, the Southwest Regional Primate Research Center, was established on June 1, 1999, at the Southwest Foundation.

Advantages of Nonhuman Primate Models in Research

Genetic and Physiological Similarities. Primates are genetically and physiologically more similar to humans than are other animal species. Use of nonhuman primate models allows investigation of complex physiological characteristics that are shared only by humans and other primates.

Infectious Disease Susceptibility Similarities. Only humans and other primates are susceptible to many of the infectious diseases that threaten human populations.

Similarities in Characteristics of the Menopause. Only humans and some nonhuman primates undergo menopause. No other animal models are available for studying health issues related to the natural onset of menopause.

Similarities in Chronic Disease Profiles. Primates more closely resemble humans than any other animal model in manifestations of the chronic diseases that are the major public health problems in the United States today. For example, nonhuman primates have naturally occurring atherosclerosis, osteoporosis and hypertension making them ideal animal models for these conditions.

Ability to Control Matings. The ability to control breeding of nonhuman primates allows experimental testing of specific genetic hypotheses that is not possible in human populations.

Ability to Control Environment. Primates can be maintained in a similar environment throughout life. The ability to control and maintain environmental factors facilitates many experimental evaluations not possible in human populations.

Alternatives to Animal Research

Many research questions only can be answered through detailed study of a whole living system. Disease processes are often complex, involving multiple physiological processes and multiple organ systems.

Primates Help Fight Hepatitis C

"Hepatitis C is a devastating disease that exacts a significant toll in this country and abroad, and whose full clinical impact has yet to be realized," states Anthony S. Fauci, M.D., director of the National Institute of Allergy and Infectious Diseases (NIAID). "This research on chimpanzees helps to explain how the virus manages to persist in the body and provides physicians with a potential way to predict the development of a chronic infection."

With these findings, and others, researchers are making collective headway in finding ways to derail the slow but insidious damage caused by hepatitis C infection. With chimpanzees as animal test subjects, we may one day have a vaccine to prevent the disease, or at least a strategy for treating its symptoms.

Foundation for Biomedical Research, "Chimpanzees: A Crucial Role in Hepatitis C Research," www.fbresearch.org/hepatitis_body.html.

While some specific research questions may be adequately addressed using cell cultures, tissue studies, or computer models, whole animal research continues to be critical for the advancement of human health.

Adjuncts to animal research, frequently termed "alternatives," can complement research using whole animals but cannot replace the need for whole animals in biomedical research on complex normal and disease-related processes.

Judicious Use of Primates in Research

The vast majority of animal research is done with mice and rats. Primates are used as research subjects only when a scientific question cannot be answered by using lower animals.

When primates must be used, the lower primates (monkeys) are used whenever possible. Chimpanzees are used only when the scientific question requires the use of a higher primate species (apes).

Use of Anesthesia in Animal Research

According to the USDA, 93 percent of research animals do not experience pain related to experimental use either because the experiments have no painful procedures associated with them (58 percent) or because anesthesia and/or painkillers are used in the experimental protocol (35 percent).

Some carefully regulated and monitored research studies (7 percent) where anesthesia or painkillers are not given are necessary for studies of chronic pain, or are necessitated when anesthesia would compromise the scientific quality of the data.

> *"Federally funded primate research centers*
> *. . . have little regard for or understanding*
> *of the animals they experiment on. Any*
> *abuse is allowed in the name of Science."*

Nonhuman Primates Should Not Be Used in Experiments

Coalition to End Primate Experimentation

The Coalition to End Primate Experimentation was founded to protest the treatment of monkeys and apes in eight federally funded Regional Primate Research Centers. The coalition maintains in the following viewpoint that nonhuman primates should not be used in experiments because they are morally equal to humans. To illustrate the unscientific nature of testing on nonhuman primates, the coalition catalogs some of what it claims are cruel and unnecessary research projects being conducted at the Primate Centers.

As you read, consider the following questions:
1. According to the coalition, who first discovered tool use in nonhuman primates?
2. What is SIB, according to the coalition?
3. According to the coalition, what kind of research is Margarete Tigges pursuing at the Yerkes Regional Primate Center?

Excerpted from "The Argument," by Coalition to End Primate Experimentation, http://cepe.enviroweb.org, 1997. Copyright © 1997 by the Coalition to End Primate Experimentation. Reprinted with permission.

In the late 1950's researchers came back from a tour in the Soviet Union. While there, they visited the Soviets' primate research facility. These scientists became alarmed that the Soviet Union was ahead of us in the biomedical race. Their trip seems to have led to James Watt, director of the National Institutes of Health, testifying before Congress about the need for a similar program in the United States if we were not to be left behind.

Closing the Gap

At that time, nearly 45 years ago, our understanding of primates was very limited and naive. Philosophers and ethicists of the time believed that the gulf between humans and other animals was wide and clearly defined: Only humans made, modified, and used tools. Only humans possessed language. Only humans possessed culture. Only humans participated in systematic warfare. Only humans could exhibit altruistic behavior. Only humans pondered death and participated in religious ritual. Monkeys and apes, while they might be something like us in appearance and biology, were nothing like us inside, in heart and mind.

Today we know that those philosophers and ethicists were completely wrong.

Tool use in primates was first discovered in 1960 by Jane Goodall. Since that time we have learned that chimpanzees use an assortment of tools. Examples of meta-tool use, using a tool to modify or improve another tool, have been documented. Capuchins, a New World species of monkey, are known tool users as well; and macaques, an Old World group, readily learn to operate computer joysticks in laboratories.

Almost 30 years ago people began to search for ways to communicate with apes and monkeys. They wondered whether real language use was even possible for non-humans. Today, many chimpanzees have been taught American Sign Language and have been engaging in dialog with humans. From these conversations it is now clear that their perceptions of the world are nearly identical to ours. They combine words to coin new expressions for novel situations and objects which we fully understand. An example of this is a chimpanzee signing, fruit drink when inventing a name for Kool-Aid. Chimpanzees, bonobos, orangutans, and gorillas have all been found to be adept at learning human language. To date, few humans have come close to learning a non-human primate language. Noam Chomsky once criticized the research in sign language saying that if chimpanzees were capable of a gestural language they would be using one in the wild. He believed that this put the matter to rest, but since then we have learned that chimpanzees do use such a language in the wild.

The discovery that chimpanzees use a gestural language in the wild has contributed to the understanding that culture is passed from generation to generation. Language and tool use are both used in unique ways between different chimpanzee groups. The knowledge of how to use a specific tool and specific gestures is learned and transmitted between generations. Rhesus macaques use at least 18 different words or phrases (calls) in the wild, but when raised in captivity, a culturally deprived setting, they learn only five or six.

War and Altruism

It has been known for eons that animals will sometimes fight with each other, but systematic warfare was considered a uniquely human trait. It is now known that chimpanzees sometimes engage in long term aggression with neighboring groups and will systematically murder each member of the "enemy" group. This is accomplished through a band of mostly males silently searching for isolated members of the rival community and killing them. Such campaigns can last months on end with frequently repeated excursions into the rivals' territory.

Altruism has long been a bastion of human uniqueness, but the frequency of adoption of orphaned babies in chimpanzee society is high. Chimpanzees are well known for their willingness to put themselves at risk to aid a friend. Gorillas will defend their group members to the death. People observing chimpanzees in the wild have been given food by them. And who did not read of the child [who had fallen into the gorilla area] saved at the Brookfield Zoo in Chicago in 1996 by Binti Jua, the captive lowland gorilla?

During a particularly violent lightning storm, Jane Goodall observed a group of chimpanzees repeatedly run down a hill one at a time brandishing a branch. After running down the hill screaming and waving the branch each chimpanzee would climb back up to repeat the performance. The group continued this ritual until the electrical storm had passed. Had an anthropologist observed the same phenomenon while studying a tribe of humans she would have likely believed it to be a religious rite.

When asked what happens to you when you die, a gorilla answered in sign, "Dark. Ground."

Today, in biomedical laboratories around the world, monkeys and apes are treated as if the past years of study mean nothing. The ethical and moral implications of what we now know about the similarities between human and non-human primates are ignored and suppressed by the National Institutes of Health and the primate labs themselves.

The Primate Research Centers

The Oregon Regional Primate Research Center: Oline K. Ronnekleiv is administering cocaine to pregnant mothers and unborn fetuses. He has discovered that chronic cocaine use causes brain damage. . . .

Washington Regional Primate Research Center: . . . Virginia M. Gunderson has received a Scientist Development Award to " . . . gain expertise. . . [and] . . . acquire the skills to attain her career goals." She is injecting chemicals into the brains of very young pigtailed macaques to try to induce seizures.

New England Regional Primate Research Center: Janice H. Kinsey designed a database to keep records on the large population of individually housed monkeys. She gathered data on the amount of various behaviors such as: ". . . pacing, bouncing, rocking, . . . self-biting, grasping, and hair pulling." She learned that 10% of the center's monkeys bite themselves. [Sometimes they chew off fingers or tail tips and chew holes in their arms that require veterinary care.]

Alyssa Rulf Fountain, studying self-injurious behavior (SIB) such as self-biting, reports that ". . . the causes are largely unknown."

Both of these studies above are ongoing, but as early as 1990 researchers had found that even a small hole between cages of individually caged monkeys which allowed them to touch each other stopped most of this behavior. Ms. Fountain's assertion notwithstanding, the cause of SIB has been well known for years: Most non-human primates are more social than humans and isolating them causes insanity.

Likes Must Be Treated Alike

Using raw power to exploit nonhuman primates *because they are like us* rests on an argument that is arbitrary, unprincipled, and corrosive to equality, which at bottom demands that likes be treated alike.

Steven M. Wise, *Rattling the Cage: Toward Legal Rights for Animals*, 2000.

Wisconsin Regional Primate Research Center: Christopher L. Coe says that, "Prior research at our laboratory has determined that stressful events experienced by the pregnant female monkey can affect her fetus . . .". Now he wants to know, ". . . whether the absence of breast milk and its soluble immune products exacerbates the effects of prenatal disturbance."

In a similar study at the Wisconsin center, researchers are scarring the amygdala (a deep brain structure) of female monkeys to induce a permanent state of fear. They want to know whether such stress can affect a baby born to such an afflicted mother.

Ridiculous and Cruel

Tulane Regional Primate Research Center: Margaret R. Clark is working to enlarge the breeding colony of rhesus macaques. She wishes the facility to produce an additional 150 babies a year. She says, " . . . infants will be removed [from their mothers and all adult monkeys] within three days of birth. . . . Management practices will maximize the psychological well-being of the animals."

Gamal M. Ghoniem is implanting vascular cuffs around the neck of the bladder of rhesus macaques. A lead to this cuff runs out of the monkeys' bodies and allows him to squeeze off the neck of the bladder while the monkeys attempt to urinate. He has found that monkeys whose bladder necks are most tightly closed take longer to pee than those with less obstruction.

Yerkes Regional Primate Research Center: Leonard L.

Howell has learned that monkeys trained to drink caffeine will self-administer lower doses than monkeys trained to receive intravenous injections.

Margarete Tigges is sewing the eyelids shut on newborn infants.

California Regional Primate Research Center: David G. Amaral is using chemical means to permanently disconnect the amygdalas from the rest of the brain in male monkeys. He wants to know whether they will still be able to communicate with facial expression. He says this will help us understand criminality and psychopathic behavior in humans.

William Gilbert is ligating (tying shut) esophagi and catheterizing the tracheas of fetus rhesus macaques. He characterizes this as chronic catheterization which means that these babies inside their mothers have these tubes in them for days or months on end.

In the Name of Science

What these examples teach is that the federally funded primate research centers around the United States have little regard for or understanding of the animals they experiment on. Any abuse is allowed in the name of Science. Studies routinely repeat experiments that have been done on humans. Monkeys are disposed of as if they are broken equipment.

Every center has received warnings about the condition of the animals' housing. Every center keeps monkeys in isolation. Every center receives over 10 million dollars a year. Expansion is underway around the country. Every law to protect and enhance the life of these animals has been heavily lobbied against by the biomedical community.

The researchers say this work is important because we learn about humans since monkeys and apes are so like us, but at the same time they say we should not be concerned over the torment these animals suffer because they are so unlike us.

Biomedical researchers have made the same arguments and done similar things to minorities throughout history. The research taking place at the NIH Regional Primate Research Centers is just more of the same. Its root cause is the bigotry that is always associated with unbridled hubris. *Only when people speak out will it end.*

> "Dogs are surgically mutilated, infected with
> dangerous viruses and made to suffer
> convulsions, vomiting and other symptoms."

Dogs Should Not Be Used for Animal Experimentation

Animal Aid

Animal Aid, an organization based in the United Kingdom, investigates and exposes animal cruelty. In the following viewpoint, the organization argues that biomedical research on dogs is unscientific and cruel. Animal Aid contends that because dogs and humans are so physically different, many drugs that have been deemed safe for human use after experimentation on dogs have turned out to be toxic to humans. In addition, the organization asserts that cruelty against laboratory dogs—including toxicity tests performed without anesthetics and physical abuse—is common.

As you read, consider the following questions:
1. How many experiments on dogs and cats are performed in the United Kingdom per year, according to Animal Aid?
2. According to Animal Aid, what non-medical substances are tested on dogs?
3. How many deaths occur per year in the United States due to the side effects of medications, according to the organization?

Companion animals are the lucky ones. There are thousands of cats and dogs who never have a loving home, never have toys to play with, never explore the garden or woods. They live in barren cages or pens, born to die as victims of science. According to the latest government figures, around 10,000 experiments 'likely to cause . . . pain, suffering, distress or lasting harm' are carried out on cats and dogs every year.

Pets Versus Research Subjects

The scientists' own published papers reveal that these animals suffer major damage to vital body systems, such as the heart, lung, brain and liver. They are surgically mutilated, infected with dangerous viruses and made to suffer convulsions, vomiting and other symptoms.

Supporters of vivisection often claim that animals in laboratories are well protected by the law. In fact, while undergoing experiments, the usual domestic anti-cruelty laws are not applicable. On the contrary, the legislation that controls vivisection sanctions the infliction of pain and suffering. It is the experimenters who are protected—from prosecution!

What is the nature of the experiments on cats and dogs? The animals are used to investigate a host of human afflictions, to see how the body works, and especially in the case of dogs, for drug and product testing. Some have even been employed in military research. Yet if similar treatment were meted out to the family cat or dog there would be outrage. This ambivalence is vividly illustrated by the well known Oxford experimenter Colin Blakemore who shared his home with a cat called Trevor. In the laboratory, however, Blakemore and his colleagues blinded numerous kittens for research into the visual system.

Victims of Science

Despite being favourite companion animals, cats and dogs are forced into battle against some of our most serious ailments—even though there is a wealth of evidence demonstrating that they make hopelessly unreliable 'models' of human beings.

Cats are used for research into stroke, whilst dogs are

commonly employed to investigate heart disease; both are used for migraine research. Experimenters try to mimic human disease by artificially inducing the condition, or its consequences, in animals. So, at the Institute of Psychiatry in London, cats were brain-damaged following a deliberately induced 'stroke', produced by blocking arteries in the animal's head. Likewise, scientists at the University of Oxford produced 'heart disease' in beagle dogs by tightening a wire around one of the coronary arteries.

Many of the experiments are commercially driven, being carried out by pharmaceutical firms to develop new drugs. In recently published examples, Glaxo-Wellcome used dogs to research yet another blood pressure pill, even though there are currently in excess of 60 available to doctors. SmithKline Beecham, Pfizer and Glaxo-Wellcome are in the lucrative migraine market, developing further drugs to combat headache. All have used dogs and, in the case of SmithKline Beecham, cats for the purpose. In other examples, companies have employed dogs to develop a heart drug (Pfizer), a cholesterol-lowering treatment (SmithKline Beecham) and an anti-thrombosis drug (Zeneca).

Analysis shows that most new drugs offer no therapeutic improvement over existing products, and are introduced for commercial reasons.

During the 1980s, the government's centre for chemical and biological warfare, Porton Down, revealed that beagle dogs were being used in cyanide poison tests. A decade later, beagles were employed to develop a new sensory irritant called I-MCHT, whose effects are similar to those of CS and CN (tear) gas. At higher doses, the dogs suffered incoordination, convulsions, trembling, hyperactivity and rapid involuntary movement of the eyeballs.

Dogs are also used for testing non-medical substances. During the 1990s, thousands of beagles have been used to test the safety of agricultural chemicals, industrial substances, food additives and household products. These experiments are carried out by chemical companies and contract research laboratories. Product testing, together with the safety assessment of new drugs, account for most of the experiments (68 per cent) on dogs. . . .

Pain and Suffering

Most experiments on dogs are conducted without any anaesthetics. Dogs are most commonly employed for toxicity tests which rarely use any form of pain relief. This is because experiments can last for weeks or months and, in any case, an anaesthetic may interfere with the test substance, so making it even more difficult to make the data relevant to people. Although the findings from safety tests are usually kept secret for commercial reasons, the United Kingdom's (UK's) Centre for Medicines Research has compiled information from industry sources which list symptoms and injuries experienced by dogs during drug trials. These included vomiting, diarrhoea, convulsions, shivering, anorexia and hyper-excitement; plus eye, liver, kidney, heart and lung damage, and of course death.

Dog Dealing

Poplar Bluff, Missouri, sits in the heart of dog-dealing country. The Midwest's interstates and local roads are conduits for a vast network that transports stolen dogs from virtually every state for sale at trade days like this one. The number of dogs that go missing each year under suspicious circumstances has been conservatively estimated by shelters and pounds, animal-protection organizations, and veterinarians to be in the hundreds of thousands. Puppy-mill breeders and the organizers of dog fights buy their share, but the animals also end up as subjects in the biomedical-research industry, which pays top dollar. Although it is impossible to know how many dogs this is, Patricia Jensen, then a former U.S. Department of Agriculture (USDA) assistant secretary, testified in 1996 that "one of the most egregious problems in research" is the "introduction of stolen and fraudulently acquired pets into the process."

Judith Reitman, *Atlantic Monthly*, July 2000.

It is not only during the experiment that animals may suffer. In March 1997 the Channel 4 television documentary Countryside Undercover revealed how two technicians at Huntingdon Life Sciences (HLS) had punched and violently shaken beagle dogs used for experiment. HLS is Europe's largest contract research laboratory and uses dogs and other animals to test products on behalf of clients. . . .

Dogs Fail Ultimate Test

The use of beagle dogs and other animals to test the safety of medicines must be seriously questioned following an American investigation which found an unexpectedly high number of side-effects. The study of hospital patients in the United States suggests that medicines could harm as many as 2.2 million people a year, causing 106,000 deaths. This would make drug-induced fatalities the fourth biggest killer behind heart disease, cancer and strokes! The findings, published during 1998 in the *Journal of the American Medical Association*, show that animal testing does not make medicines safe for human use.

The most serious side-effects of oral contraceptives are on the circulatory system, placing women at increased risk of blood clots. Animal tests not only failed to identify the problems, but in dogs, the pill had totally the opposite effect, making it more difficult for their blood to clot! Mitoxantrone was developed in the hope of providing effective anti-cancer treatment without side-effects on the heart. In experiments with beagles, the drug appeared safe but in clinical practice, cardiac toxicity proved to be a major problem, with several patients suffering heart failure. And for years the contraceptive Depo-Provera was denied to many women because dogs falsely predicted fatal side-effects. . . .

Dogs in Heart Research

Dogs are commonly used to investigate the causes and consequences of heart disease. An unconvincing version of the human ailment is introduced by tying off, or otherwise blocking, blood vessels to the dog's heart.

The illogicality of using dogs for heart disease research was underlined by William Clifford Roberts, editor in chief of *The American Journal of Cardiology*.

'Although human beings eat meat we are not natural carnivores,' he wrote in an editorial. 'No matter how much fat carnivores eat, they do not develop atherosclerosis,' Roberts added. 'It is virtually impossible, for example, to produce atherosclerosis in a dog even when 100 grams of cholesterol and 120 grams of butter fat are added to its meat ration. (This amount of cholesterol is approximately 200 times the average amount that human beings in the USA eat each day!) In contrast, herbivores rapidly develop atherosclerosis if they are fed foods, namely fat and cholesterol, intended for natural carnivores. . . . And humans are like rabbits, natural herbivores.'. . . .

Experiments Should Be Stopped

The fact that cats and dogs are the most popular companion animals does not protect them from the vivisection industry. It is intolerable that animals cherished by so many can be so ruthlessly exploited by the few. Do scientists and dealers really think that cats and dogs bred for research feel less or have less right to life than the family friend?

We are convinced that the British public will be horrified by the revelations contained in this report. Our view is that such experiments should be stopped immediately. We call for a full-scale government inquiry into the use of cats and dogs for research and testing.

| *"Although dogs represent less than 1 percent of the animals used in biomedical research each year, their contributions to various fields of medicine are numerous."*

Experiments on Dogs Have Led to Medical Breakthroughs

Foundation for Biomedical Research

In the following viewpoint, the Foundation for Biomedical Research contends that because a dog's physiology is in many ways similar to a human's, dogs make excellent research models. The organization asserts that using dogs in biomedical research allows scientists to practice new surgical techniques, train emergency personnel, and test the toxicity of various substances. According to the foundation, such experimentation on dogs has led to many important medical breakthroughs. The Foundation for Biomedical Research provides information on what it sees as the necessary and important role of laboratory animals in research.

As you read, consider the following questions:
1. What made heart operations possible, according to the foundation?
2. According to the foundation, what potentially harmful substance have dogs been especially useful in studying?
3. What laid the foundation for behavioral research, according to the organization?

A lthough dogs represent less than 1 percent of the animals used in biomedical research each year, their contributions to various fields of medicine are numerous. What follows are some examples of recent and ongoing research using dogs.

Heart and Lungs

Because their cardiovascular and respiratory systems resemble those of a human being, dogs have been instrumental to our current understanding of the functions and diseases of these organs.

- Researchers have developed a process to stop and restart a dog's heartbeat. This was the first step in making it possible to operate on the heart.
- Research on dogs led to development of the heart-lung machine, which allows surgeons to sustain life while performing heart surgery.
- Heart surgery techniques, such as coronary bypass surgery, artificial heart valve insertion, and pacemaker implantation, were tested and studied in dogs before being used in humans.
- Research with dogs has made it possible to correct the defect that causes blue babies. This surgical procedure corrects a congenital error in development of the large vessels connecting the heart to the lungs.
- Procedures for treating emphysema were made possible through research on dogs.
- Dogs were vital to the development of angioplasty, in which a small tube is threaded up through the femoral artery to unblock coronary arteries.

Organ Transplants

Dogs were the first animal used in the attempt to conquer rejection during organ transplantation. The 1990 Nobel Prize for medicine was awarded to researchers who studied the immunologic basis of organ rejection by working with dogs. These studies resulted in the ability to transplant kidneys, hearts, lungs, livers and pancreases in human patients.

Diabetes

Through the use of dogs, researchers found that diabetics lack the hormone insulin. Surgeons are studying methods of transplanting the insulin-producing cells of the pancreas to extend and improve diabetics' quality of life and treat complications accompanying the disease. They have already succeeded in transplanting an artificial pancreas into dogs, which they hope can lead to a permanent treatment in humans.

Rules for Using Unwanted Dogs in Research

Using dogs which would otherwise be killed in pounds can obviate the need to breed additional dogs for research. However, investigators should be aware of community concern about the use of pound dogs in medical research. One of the major issues is the length of time allowed to claim dogs from local pounds and the concern that family pets may be included inadvertently along with unwanted stray dogs as experimental animals in medical research.

In order to allay community fears:

a. It is essential that institutions know about local government and State laws relating to the use of pound dogs in medical research and that these laws are followed strictly.

b. When animals are obtained from a public pound:

   i. Dogs must be held by the research institution for a minimum of seven days in addition to any statutory requirements placed on pounds. Isolation should be avoided if possible. . . .

   ii. Institutions must maintain full records of every dog obtained from a pound and these records must indicate the identification number given to the dog by the pound. After issue by the institution, the maintenance of adequate records becomes the responsibility of the investigator.

   iii. Dogs carrying identification given to them by the owner, including microchips, must not be used (except to obtain post mortem material), unless the written consent of the owner has been obtained.

National Health and Medical Research Council, "NHMRC Policy on the Care of Dogs Used for Scientific Purposes."

Trauma and Shock

Dogs are used to train emergency room physicians and nurses in lifesaving techniques to be used in trauma patients.

Studies in dogs for post-shock infections, heart complications, kidney function, blood pressure levels and anesthesia techniques have allowed doctors to correct previously irreversible conditions.

Skeletal System

Through research on dogs, scientists have gained extensive information on repairing fractured bones and saving the limbs of humans. The artificial hip was developed in dogs and led to the invention of the current array of replacement and repair techniques for many types of joints, such as artificial knees and knuckles. Cartilage and tendon repair and the fusion of spinal vertebrae are among the procedures developed in dogs that now benefit humans and animals.

Anesthesia

Dogs are used to evaluate anesthesia equipment and methods and to evaluate anesthetic/tranquilizing agents. Research with dogs also has resulted in design improvements in equipment used for maintaining a constant flow of oxygen through the lungs during anesthesia in dogs and humans.

Microsurgery

Research on dogs has advanced and improved microsurgery, which has been vital to reattaching toes, fingers and arms that have been severed.

Gastrointestinal System

Research on the gastrointestinal tract of dogs has allowed surgeons to remove, reconstruct and mend the colon, intestine and abdominal organs.

Toxicity

Dogs are exposed to certain products to determine what levels may be harmful or dangerous to human beings and what is the best treatment. Dogs have been especially useful in studying the harmful effects of radiation.

Behavioral Research

- Pavlov's studies of dog physiology and psychology laid the foundation for behavioral research. Knowledge acquired through these studies has been transferred to hu-

man behavioral analysis.
- Behavioral studies made possible the training of guard dogs and dogs used to aid those who are blind and deaf.
- Dogs have been useful for studying anorexia nervosa and other psychological traumas associated with food.

Neurological Diseases

A colony of Brittany Spaniels has been developed to serve as a model for amyotrophic lateral sclerosis (ALS), commonly known as Lou Gehrig's disease, which destroys nerves in the brain and spinal cord and strikes about 5,000 Americans a year. The dogs have an inherited disease that produces progressive paralysis similar to that found in human ALS. Studies of the canine disease show that it is inherited as a dominant trait, as are some cases of the human disease. Because dogs can reproduce quickly, genetic studies can provide insights that would be difficult to study in humans.

Animal Diseases

Studies in dogs have led to the development of devices and treatments for animals, including pacemakers, hip and artificial joint replacements, diabetes treatments, dental care, chemotherapy and canine vaccines for diseases such as rabies.

"The exclusion of rats and mice in the Animal Welfare Act 'leaves significant loopholes in the law's effectiveness and is detrimental to the excluded animals' welfare.'"

Rats and Mice Should Be Included in the Animal Welfare Act

F. Barbara Orlans

In the following viewpoint, F. Barbara Orlans asserts that a major shortcoming of the Animal Welfare Act—which was passed in 1966 to protect the welfare of laboratory animals—is its exclusion of rats and mice. Orlans contends that rats, mice, and birds constitute 90 percent of all animals used in laboratory research, and since these animals feel pain in the same way that animals included in the act do, they should be similarly protected. F. Barbara Orlans is a senior research fellow at the Kennedy Institute of Ethics.

As you read, consider the following questions:
1. According to Orlans, what requirements do the Animal Welfare Act impose on scientists conducting research on animals covered by the law?
2. In the author's opinion, what species included in the Animal Welfare Act are similar to mice and rats?
3. What are the "Three R's," according to Orlans?

Excerpted from "The Injustice of Excluding Laboratory Rats, Mice, and Birds from the Animal Welfare Act," by F. Barbara Orlans, *Kennedy Institute of Ethics Journal*, September 2000. Copyright © 2000 by Johns Hopkins University Press. Reprinted with permission.

The first law to establish humane standards for laboratory animals used in biomedical experimentation was passed by Congress in 1966. Since then, it has been strengthened several times by amendments. The most recent amendments were in 1985 when sweeping new provisions, such as protocol review by Institutional Animal Care [and Use] Committees (Animal Welfare Act 1985), became law. This law, which is administered by the U.S. Department of Agriculture (USDA), has contributed significantly to improving the welfare of laboratory animals. It requires that investigators who use certain named species must: (1) register with the USDA and be open to inspection by government officials; (2) comply with humane provisions such as adequate housing for the animals; and (3) where possible, minimize or eliminate animal pain and distress, and so on.

Shortcomings in the Animal Welfare Act

However, a major shortcoming of the original act has not yet been remedied. It excludes the most-used species—rats, mice, and birds. The species that *are* covered by the Animal Welfare Act (AWA) include primates, dogs, cats, rabbits, gerbils, and certain other animals. But, based on data from large U.S. research institutions, the excluded species comprise 90 percent of all animals used in laboratory research. Their exclusion leaves significant loopholes in the law's effectiveness and is detrimental to the excluded animals' welfare. No action by Congress is needed to reverse this exclusion: rather USDA needs to revise its rule making, which is the administrative agency's mechanism for enforcing the law.

Repeated endeavors by the public to pressure USDA to tighten the law to include all species have, until recently, failed. But a petition filed 29 April 1999 to USDA to include rats, mice, and birds may be more successful. The petition was spearheaded by Alternatives Research and Development Foundation (a branch of the American Anti-Vivisection Society) and some individuals, including myself. USDA published and responded to the petition, and solicited public comment (Federal Register 1999). As of August 2000, the comment period is now closed. The next move will be USDA's public announcement of amended rules on species covered under the AWA.[1]

The United States is probably the largest user of laboratory animals in the world and holds an influential position in the international scientific community. It is also the only country that excludes these most-used species from its animal protection laws. It is an internationally embarrassing anomaly that the U.S. law is so deficient, and it sets a poor example for countries that look to the U.S. to set standards regarding scientific work. . . .

Ethical Considerations: Justice

The principle of justice is violated by the exclusion of these three species from the AWA. Justice is a major ethical principle for assessing what is right or wrong. It instructs us, to some extent, that consistency is a hallmark of the ethical life when the circumstances are similar. To amplify the issue of justice, I will offer arguments concerning: (1) the comparative *moral standings* of certain species; (2) the *perception of pain* by the excluded species; and (3) the injustice of *depriving selected animals from the positive benefits of inclusion under the law*.

Moral Standing

It is a matter of justice that animals of similar moral worth be treated equally. To justify any dissimilar treatment, there has to be a difference in some morally relevant characteristic. Whatever views are held about the relative moral standing of different species of animals overall, I suggest that two of the excluded species—mice and rats—are so similar to three included species—hamsters, guinea pigs, and gerbils—that it is arbitrary, against common sense, and unjust to exclude the former from legal protection.

Indeed, all five species, mice, rats, hamsters, guinea pigs, and gerbils, are similar in many ways. All are widely used and are commercially purpose-bred for research, and physiologically and anatomically they are, to a large extent, commensurable. Furthermore, and importantly from an ethical stand-

1. In October 2000, the U.S. Department of Agriculture reached a settlement with the Alternatives Research and Development Foundation to include mice, rats, and birds in the Animal Welfare Act. However, budgetary restraints and protests from researchers have delayed the change until October 2001.

point, the burdens they bear as subjects of biomedical experiments are of the same order: as discussed in the following section, they have similar sensibilities in their perception of pain, and all are likely to be killed before the end of their normal life-span. If any of these species have an interest in not being subjected to pain or suffering and not having their lives prematurely foreshortened, then they *all* do. Inasmuch as there must be some morally relevant difference between individuals to justify different treatment of them, there is no justification for the dissimilar treatment in terms of legal protection of the animals excluded from the AWA.

Animals' Capacity to Perceive Pain

Mice and rats are as capable of perceiving pain as the animal species that *are* covered by the AWA, such as other rodents. One cannot argue that mice and rats are excluded because they feel less pain than other species. Furthermore, perception of pain by mice and rats bears significant resemblance to that of humans. Indeed, this is why mice and rats are used extensively in research to develop new anesthetics for humans. The research results show that they are good models: in gen-

© Luckovich. Reprinted by permission of Creators Syndicate.

eral, anesthetics that work for mice and rats also work for humans. Post-surgically, mice and rats will self-administer analgesics in just the same way that humans do. Although research suggests that mice and rats may not suffer mentally to the same extent that humans do, they do perceive physical pain that is comparable to that of humans and they do experience adverse mental states such as fear and anxiety. What physically hurts a human being hurts a mouse or a rat—or a bird for that matter. Perception of pain in birds is well-recognized. Nationally-accepted humane standards for birds require that anesthetics be used for surgical procedures. Insofar as the degree (duration and severity) of pain inflicted on laboratory animals is *the* primary ethical concern in using animals for human benefit and a primary reason for protecting any species of animal, the exclusion of certain species that possess similar capabilities of pain perception is both irrational and unjust.

Exclusions from Benefits of the Law: The Three R's

Another issue involves the AWA's requirement to consider the "Three R alternatives" to promote a more humane use of animals in research. The Three R's are: *refinement* of procedures to minimize or eliminate animal pain; *reduction* in the numbers of animals used; and *replacement*, where possible, of animal use with non-animal alternatives. Practical application of the Three R's, which occurs to a significant extent as a result of the AWA's mandatory protocol review process, is a matter of importance because it improves animal welfare and provides a standard by which to compare experimental results from different laboratories. Without mandatory protocol review, application of the Three R's can be weakened and some investigators are free of a legal obligation to apply the Three R's. The exclusion of mice, rats, and birds from coverage under the act therefore reduces the effectiveness of the Three R alternatives requirement, which negatively affects these animals.

Furthermore, since application of the Three R's is a major way to reduce the harms to animals used in experimentation, it is a matter of considerable public interest that a national assessment be made over the years to see how well they are being applied. But since only about 10 percent of all laboratory animals used in research in the U.S. are reported in the official national statistics and inadequate questions are asked about how much welfare compromise is involved in the experiments, assessment of trends in refinement, reduction, and replacement is not possible. However, in countries where all species subject to experimentation are covered by animal welfare laws and where official data are reported about the degree of welfare compromise resulting from the animal experiments, it is possible to track a decline in experiments that involve severe animal harm. Since all animals are counted, reduction in (and to some extent replacement of) animal use can be measured with confidence. As for tracking refinements, the key is to categorize the relative harms inflicted by different experiments, grading them as either minor, moderate, or severe. The harms that result from experimental procedures include many things such as distress (nausea, anxiety, fatigue); pain; induced pathological conditions, such as infectious diseases; functional disability, such as loss of a limb; maternal or social deprivation; and induced adverse mental states.

In the six countries that mandate the grading of such harms—Canada, Finland, The Netherlands, New Zealand, Switzerland, and the United Kingdom—a consensus is developed by the oversight committees of how to categorize the various procedures and the modifying factors to be considered. In both Switzerland and The Netherlands, there has been a diminution in the number of animal experiments falling within the severe harm category. In addition, the number of animals used in experimentation in The Netherlands has dropped by about half, from 1,242,285 in 1984 to 618,432 in 1997. This demonstrates that there has, indeed, been progress in the application of the Three R's, a matter of significant public interest and satisfaction. The official data of these and other countries provide greater public accountability on animal experimentation than do the data available in the U.S. Indeed, USDA's mandated annual reports on animal experimentation are largely ignored by Congress and the public because of deficiencies of the data. . . .

The exclusion of rats, mice, and birds is a significant loophole in the law that should be closed. In my view, no experimental work involving animal harm should proceed without legal oversight for the protection of the animals' welfare. Unless action is taken now by USDA, the biotechnology industry may well grow beyond control, and the welfare of many animals will suffer immeasurably. Justice dictates that this opportunity to do the right thing not be missed.

"Nice people stand up for [mice and rats] in the lab. They don't think about the nice, but sick, human beings who are helped by animal research."

Including Mice and Rats in the Animal Welfare Act Would Hinder Research

Debra J. Saunders

Debra J. Saunders argues in the following viewpoint that rats and mice should not be included in the Animal Welfare Act. According to Saunders, although animal rights activists have reached a settlement with the U.S. Department of Agriculture to include mice and rats in the Act, current budgetary constraints and protestations from researchers have delayed the change. She maintains that federal law already protects mice and rats, and asserts that additional protections will only make research into human diseases more difficult. Debra J. Saunders is a columnist for the *San Francisco Chronicle*.

As you read, consider the following questions:

1. What human diseases does Saunders list to show that experimentation on rats and mice is vital?
2. According to the author, how quickly do mice reproduce?
3. What percentage of the rats and mice in the United States are bred for pet food, according to Saunders?

I n an era when political activists only want to speak on is-sues that make them look like nice people—save the whales, don't cut old redwood trees—few are eager to push for policies that facilitate medical research with lab animals.

Helping Minnie Mouse

Nice people don't want to experiment on Minnie Mouse. Nice people want to tell researchers to be kind to lab rats and mice. Nice people stand up for their furry friends in the lab. They don't think about the nice, but sick, human beings who are helped by animal research. Thinking about people gets in the way.

This makes it all the more startling that an institution of higher learning, Johns Hopkins University in Baltimore, has risked playing the villain in order to facilitate life-saving medical research.

"If you have a child with cystic fibrosis, or juvenile diabetes, if you have a parent with Alzheimer's, this is your fight," Hopkins' general counsel Estelle Fishbein explained. Add Parkinson's, Lou Gehrig's disease, AIDS and breast cancer.

Johns Hopkins went to court to try to stop a court settlement reached in October 2000 by former President Clinton's Department of Agriculture and animal rights activists [the Alternatives Research and Development Foundation, a branch of the Anti-Vivisection Society]. That agreement sweeps lab rats, mice and birds under the protection of the Animal Welfare Act.

The animal rights people like to argue that they only want to ensure that rats and mice are treated well. Don't believe it.

"The one thing that is really consistent in their behavior is they never tell the whole story," Fishbein says. "They never tell the truth. The truth is, regulations and standards for humane compassionate care have been in place for years and years and years. . . . They make it appear that there are no standards."

Besides, common sense should tell you that sickly and mistreated rodents don't make for good research. Scientists looking for a cure for disease are less likely to find it with animals who are malnourished or living in filth.

It's not as if anyone is advocating mistreating research mice and rats—although I personally wouldn't mind if they kill all the pigeons they can find—in the name of medical science.

A Research Killer

Hopkins sees the paperwork required by the Animal Welfare Act as a research killer.

It is one thing to require labs to keep census data on laboratory cats and dogs, as the act requires, but mice are a different animal. They can produce litters every 21 days and live for only two or three years. Hopkins has 42,000 mice, 3,000 rats and 300 birds. The university is investing in a facility that will allow it to keep up to 140,000 rodents, many of them "transgenic mice" that model the symptoms of human diseases.

Rodent Protection Costs Money

[Compliance with the Animal Welfare Act for mice and rats] will likely increase [research] costs by $84 million, an investment that would not actually benefit animals. In addition, if the animal definition is revised, academic institutions and research-related companies that house only rats, mice, or birds will have to register with the U.S. Department of Agriculture (USDA) for the first time and spend as much as $80 million to $200 million to comply with all statutory requirements.

Frankie L. Trull and Barbara A. Rich, *Science*, May 28, 1999.

Imagine the unholy task of cataloging that many rodents. It's not *101 Dalmatians*. What a waste of time and energy.

A federal appropriations bill stalled the change until October 2001, but if the Bush administration does not reverse course, bureaucrats will soon be pushing to make sure that the little critters are living well. But that's already in researchers' interests—while more than 90 percent of the rats and mice bred in the United States are bred as pet food.

The settlement is the result of a lawsuit filed by a college student who complained that she was "personally, aesthetically, emotionally and profoundly disturbed"—I'll agree with that—by seeing "rats that were suffering and subject to deplorable living conditions." If true, those living conditions were still better than residing in a snake's stomach.

Watching a rat become breakfast for a snake—as is nature's way—probably doesn't enhance an observer personally, aesthetically or emotionally either.

Frankie Trull, president of the National Association for Biomedical Research in Washington, hopes the Bush administration will kill the negotiated settlement. That would spare taxpayers the expense of the Hopkins lawsuit, as well as the $18,000 the government agreed to pay the rat-huggers' attorneys.

Most importantly, if the administration drops the settlement, researchers will embark on projects without fear of silly regulations slowing them down. They'll be able to save lives sooner.

So let nice people stand up for their furry friends. Let them feel righteous. Just so long as you know that they do so at the expense of healing sick children and ailing adults.

Periodical Bibliography

The following articles have been selected to supplement the diverse views presented in this chapter. Addresses are provided for periodicals not indexed in the *Readers' Guide to Periodical Literature*, the *Alternative Press Index*, the *Social Sciences Index*, or the *Index to Legal Periodicals and Books*.

Lawrence Carter-Long "Retirement for Animals Used in Research: A Difficult Decision," *Animal Issues*, Fall 1998.

John P. Gluck "Has Anything Really Changed?" *AV Magazine*, Winter 1998.

Robert Hubrecht "Dogs and Dog Housing," www.nalusda.gov/awic/pubs/enrich/dogs.htm.

Warren E. Leary "Panel Seeks Care for Research Chimps," *New York Times*, July 17, 1997.

John McArdle "Down On the Ol' Biomedical Farm," *AV Magazine*, Summer 1997.

John McArdle "Rodent Research: Relevant or Ridiculous?" *AV Magazine*, Spring 1998.

Rachel Nowak "Almost Human," *New Scientist*, February 13, 1999.

Brenda Peterson "On the Highwire," *MSN UnderWire*, http://underwire.msn.com/underwire/social/HiWire/108Hwire.asp.

Debra J. Saunders "Rat-Huggers Are Inhumane to People," *San Francisco Chronicle*, October 10, 2000.

Wisconsin Regional Primate Center "Primates in Biomedical Research: Discoveries Through Primate Models," www.primate.wisc.edu/pin/research/contribs.html.

CHAPTER 4

Should Scientists Pursue New Forms of Animal Testing?

Chapter Preface

In 1996, Ian Wilmut, Keith Campbell, and their colleagues at Roslin Institute and PPL Therapeutics in Scotland cloned a sheep named Dolly. Dolly—the first mammal to be cloned from a single adult cell—sparked a heated controversy. Although most people are concerned about the ethics of human cloning, others worry about how cloning will impact animals. One area of particular concern is "pharming," a process whereby farm animals are made to produce medically useful compounds such as the enzyme AAT, which is used to treat the lungs of patients with emphysema. Cloning would finally enable scientists to make copies of such genetically altered animals—called transgenics—in order to produce such compounds more efficiently.

Proponents of pharming contend that it could benefit human health. For example, Ian Wilmut claims that the human protein Factor IX—a blood-clotting protein used to treat hemophilia in human patients—could be manufactured in adult sheep. Steve Jones, genetics professor at University College in London, argues that pharming cloned animals "is an extremely efficient way to make drugs." He explains, "you could make one of these transgenic sheep and then just clone it—make as many copies as you like—to create an immortal pharmaceutical factory."

However, those concerned about animal welfare argue that cloning "pharm animals" will result in an increase in cruel and unnecessary animal experiments. The American Anti-Vivisection Society argues that Dolly's creation "was the first step in the mass production of animals as 'bioreactors.'" Ingrid Newkirk, president of People for the Ethical Treatment of Animals, claims that it is not "ethical to treat animals like test tubes with tails." Those opposed to pharming contend that it is unnecessary since all of the compounds created in such experiments could be produced using non-animal methods.

Cloning genetically modified animals to produce medicine is only one of many projects which genetic engineers are currently working on. The authors in the following chapter debate whether scientists should pursue these new forms of animal testing.

*"For the first time, we can understand
exactly what has gone wrong in human
genetic diseases . . . [and] develop ways of
correcting the faults."*

Genetic Engineering Can Cure Human Diseases

Kevin O'Donnell

Kevin O'Donnell is a molecular biologist. In the following
viewpoint, O'Donnell argues that biotechnology has the potential to develop cures for all human genetic diseases. According to O'Donnell, bioengineers can manipulate the
genes of an animal to produce a gene that when implanted
into a seriously ill human will make that patient well.
O'Donnell also claims that genetically altered animals can
be cloned for use as research models or as organ donors.

As you read, consider the following questions:

1. According to O'Donnell, what were some of the first
   examples of biotechnology?
2. How many genes does the human body have, according
   to the author?
3. According to O'Donnell, what is a transgenic animal?

B iotechnology has the reputation of being very new and high tech. In fact, it is possibly the oldest technology known to man! Amongst the earliest signs of civilisation is evidence of fermentation to produce alcoholic drink. Beer and wine depend on yeast (a living micro-organism) to convert sugar into alcohol, and yeast is also used to make bread. Antibiotics are products of biotechnology. Penicillin is still produced by growing the mould that produces it, *Penicillium*, and extracting the antibiotic.

Old and New

It's the same with genetic engineering, just take a look at any domestic pet or farm animal. All are the result of many centuries of selective and deliberate breeding by humans, resulting in animals very different from those found in the wild. In other words they are the products of genetic engineering, albeit of a crude type. So, if biotechnology and genetic engineering have been around so long, why all the fuss now? The reason is that we can now do so much more.

Imagine if surgeons were compelled to carry out operations wearing boxing gloves and using blunt instruments. It would certainly limit the number of useful things they could do. Until relatively recently, biotechnology has been in exactly that position. However, tools have now been developed which allow biotechnologists to take off those boxing gloves and pick up some very sharp, very precise instruments.

We can now change living systems in much more subtle and specific ways than the crude methods allowed us to before. Although the new methods make minute changes to the genes in animals and plants, the beneficial effects are potentially much more far-reaching.

Biotechnology: The Basics

When we read we begin with ABC, but with biotechnology we begin with DNA which is found in the nucleus of every living cell. DNA is the chemical which contains all the information needed to make a complete copy of an organism— that's how a whole animal can grow from a single fertilised egg. Of course, just having the genetic information doesn't mean that we can actually make copies of living things—that would be like building a machine simply using a list of its components. It's more complicated than that. However, the first stage is to understand the genetic code.

James Watson and Francis Crick's discovery in 1953 of the structure of DNA—the double helix—led rapidly to the uncovering of how this structure contained inherited information—the genetic code. The genetic code is beautifully simple—and is the same in every living thing from bacteria to humans. This last point is very important, because it is the basis for many of the medical uses of biotechnology.

The code consists of 4 'letters' (held together by a 'backbone' of sugar phosphate); adenine, guanine, thymine and cytosine—usually abbreviated to A, G, T and C. These letters combine in different sequences to form words, each 3 letters long. Each word codes for a different amino acid. The cellular machinery reads the DNA and converts the series of words into a series of amino acids. The finished series of amino acids forms a protein. This could be a hormone, like insulin; a structural building block, like myosin, which is an important part of muscle; or an enzyme, a type of protein that catalyses or regulates one of the thousands of different chemical reactions that make up the body's metabolism. The sequence of DNA that codes for a protein is called a gene.

The human body has around 100,000 different genes, coding for proteins that may consist of several hundred amino acids. There is obviously enormous scope for something to go wrong and the amazing thing is that it hardly ever does. However, as we know only too well, it sometimes happens.

Faulty DNA

If someone has faulty DNA—sometimes as seemingly trivial as one DNA letter wrong—this leads to the wrong amino acid being inserted into a protein and this can mean that the protein is unable to carry out its normal function. The result is that individuals develop genetic diseases like Duchenne muscular dystrophy, Pompe's disease or cystic fibrosis.

So we now know the molecular basis of genetic information, and how it can go wrong. We also know how to make small changes to the DNA of animals and plants in order to change their characteristics. For the first time, we can understand exactly what has gone wrong in human genetic diseases—and that means that we have been able to develop ways of correcting the faults.

It is this new knowledge that scientists have used to breathe new life into that oldest of sciences, biotechnology.

The New Biotechnology

Essentially, the new tools which allow us to change the genetic make-up of animals (transgenic animals) allow us to do several types of things of potential benefit to patients.

Gene therapy enables doctors to change the genes in our own cells, to correct the types of mistakes and mutations, which cause disease.

We can also change animals in ways that lead to new treatments for humans through gene pharming and xeno-transplantation.

Gene Therapy

The reasoning behind gene therapy is simple. If a disease is caused by faulty genes, i.e. DNA that doesn't code for the correct amino acids, then why not replace the faulty genes with copies that work? So far, so simple. But how do we do it?

First of all, we need a copy of the gene. This is the essential first step but has been difficult. The reason is that there are around 100,000 different genes in humans. For many diseases, the genes responsible are unknown. Thankfully, this is changing—and changing fast. The Human Genome Project is an international project, involving scientists in many countries. The object is to produce a complete map of all of the genes that make up humans, including the sequence of 'letters' for each gene. This has led to many more genes being identified and associated with different diseases.[1]

Once we know what the gene is, it needs to be cloned. 'Cloning' is one of those words that seems to crop up everywhere these days, and in different contexts. Many people are confused when they hear of DNA being cloned and then also of animals being cloned. How can such different things all be

---

1. In June 2000, a working draft of the entire human genome sequence was announced by scientists working on the Human Genome Project.

clones? The reason is that 'clone' simply means 'copy', and to clone something just means to make exact copies of it. Gardeners do this all the time when they take cuttings from a plant and grow them. Our gardens are full of clones!

In the case of genes, cloning means that a copy of the gene is taken from a sample of human or animal DNA and inserted into a yeast, bacteria or virus. This allows many copies of the gene to be easily made, and used in more complicated ways.

Good Genes

What we are talking about here is getting enough copies of a "good gene" so that it can be used to treat patients who are suffering from diseases caused by a "bad" version of the same gene. Once we have enough copies of the gene, we need to get it into the right cells in the patient, and make sure it produces the required "good" protein in sufficient quantities. This has turned out to be the most difficult step of all. The gene has to be manipulated: It needs various other bits of DNA attached to it to make sure that this happens, and it needs some sort of vehicle to carry it into the target cells in the body. It should be stressed that all gene therapy being developed at the moment is somatic gene therapy. This means that it is designed to change only the body's ordinary cells. Germ-line therapy—changing the DNA of eggs, sperm or embryo so that offspring will also contain the new DNA—is not being developed because not enough is known about possible adverse effects in future generations. Two main approaches for getting DNA into humans have been tried—viruses and liposomes. The idea of using viruses to cure diseases may sound strange—after all, they cause them! Well, think about what viruses are and what they do; they are small particles which contain nucleic acid and gain entry to the cells in the body by infecting them. This makes viruses good candidates for use in gene therapy—since that is exactly what we want to do: get DNA into cells. The idea is that if the viral DNA can be replaced with the useful human DNA, then the virus could infect the body with the good gene, rather than a disease causing gene.

In fact, it has been suggested that a modified version of the AIDS virus, HIV, would be useful for this. However, viruses are not the only potential vehicle for gene therapy; scientists are also looking at the use of liposomes. These are essentially tiny globules of fat—the same sort of fat as surrounds cells—with DNA inside. The liposomes fuse with cells and release their DNA into them. These are thought to be a potentially gentler way of introducing genes to the lungs for instance, than using viruses.

Transgenic Animals

Not surprisingly, scientists are very cautious about treating patients with novel technologies such as gene therapy—especially since they might cause infection which could make patients worse, not better. After all, how would you like you, or your child, to be the first person to try an untested modified form of HIV?

Pigs as Drug Factories

Exactly one year after her own birth, Genie, our experimental sow, was serenely nursing seven healthy piglets, her milk providing the many nutrients these offspring needed to survive and grow. But unlike other pigs, Genie's milk also contained a substance that some seriously ill people desperately need: Human protein C. Traditional methods of obtaining such blood proteins for patients involve processing large quantities of donated human blood or culturing vast numbers of cells in giant stainless-steel reactor vessels. Yet Genie was producing copious amounts of protein C without visible assistance. She was the world's first pig to produce a human protein in her milk.

William H. Velander et al., *Scientific American*, January 1, 1997.

Fortunately, biotechnology has also supplied an answer to this problem. Using the new technology it has been possible to develop transgenic animals (mostly mice) with specific diseases and use them as models for developing gene therapy and other treatments for genetic diseases. All mammals have many genes in common and mutations in the same genes cause similar, if not identical, diseases—and as we know, all genes are written in the same language, regardless of where they're from.

By developing these special transgenic animals, it may be

possible in future to reduce the overall numbers of animals used in biomedical research, since they are specially adapted for research use and will give results more quickly. It also means that many genetic diseases can be properly studied for the first time. One of the biggest barriers to the development of treatments for genetic diseases has been their rarity —it is difficult to develop treatments for a disease that affects 5 children a year in the United Kingdom (UK), for example. Thanks to biotechnology, treatments can now be developed using transgenic mice with the same disease.

Gene therapy is not yet at the stage where patients are being cured—though a number of clinical trials are underway at the moment. Yet already there have been a few encouraging reports of successful gene transfer. This is a very young science—the first attempts at gene therapy were in the early 1990s. It is remarkable that so much progress has taken place, so quickly. In large part this is due to the success of using genetically engineered or transgenic animal models.

So that's what the new biotechnology is allowing us to do by changing the DNA of humans and animals. Obviously the potential for treatments for the 5,000 named genetic diseases is huge and a source of hope for many sufferers.

Gene 'Pharming'

Aside from developing models for human genetic diseases, there are two other main reasons why changing the DNA of animals could be useful—and both are at an even more advanced stage than gene therapy. The first one is making animals produce medically useful compounds: 'pharming.' This is done by cloning the human gene into animals. Why not just use tissue cultures to get the product we want? One reason is that cells don't produce much of the products of most genes. Since there are many different types of cells, each only makes products from a proportion of genes. Genes come with additional information that tells the cell when it should be used to make protein and how much should be made.

In tissue culture there is only one type of cell, and it is not always possible to persuade them to produce large amounts of the desired protein. It is also costly—an important factor when considering producing treatments for rare diseases.

One reason that cell culture is so costly is that it has a requirement for highly specified animal-derived ingredients such as fetal calf serum. So how could we use biotechnology to get around these problems? The answer is brilliantly simple. Animals make a lot of the types of protein that are produced in milk. So one approach is to clone the desired gene into an animal, along with additional genetic information that says 'produce a lot of this protein in milk.' This is a good way of producing large amounts of the desired protein, since instead of an expensive tissue culture process, dependent on animal culture, we have a living animal. Grass gets fed in and milk is produced containing valuable proteins in large amounts.

The difficulty is in producing the genetically engineered animals in the first place. This is done by inserting the human gene into embryonic cells, then implanting them into the wombs of mother animals where they grow and are born in the normal way. Then a second problem arises. If we have only one sheep, say, producing this valuable milk then how can we ensure continued supply, or increase the supply, of the milk?

Hello Dolly

This is where cloning comes into the picture again. Only instead of producing copies of a gene, we can produce copies of whole animals. This is what has been done with Dolly, the famous sheep [which was cloned in 1996 by Ian Wilmut and Keith Campbell]. Such cloning involves taking a single cell from the 'parent' animal. Scientists discovered a way in which this single cell could be persuaded to develop and grow into a new animal—just like a fertilised egg does. The difference is that the new animal is an exact copy of one 'parent.' So if the 'parent' produces a valuable pharmaceutical compound in its milk, so does the clone. Cloning is a good way of making the genetically modified founder animals for a flock producing therapeutic compounds.

Already 'pharming' is being used to produce some potentially valuable treatments for conditions like cystic fibrosis, haemophilia, emphysema and Pompe's disease. Yet there is fierce opposition from anti-vivisectionists who have concentrated on the negative aspects of the cloning technology such as surgical interventions and low survival rates. They certainly cannot attack it on animal husbandry grounds—such animals are just like ordinary farm animals—except that, as they are much more valuable, they are arguably much better looked after.

Xenotransplantation

Another exciting, and potentially life-saving, use of genetically engineered animals is in xenotransplantation. This means using organs from animals to replace diseased ones in humans, instead of using donated human organs.

The big problem with transplantation is that demand for organs far outstrips supply. A solution is to change the genetic code of animals such as pigs so that their organs are more acceptable to the human immune system. This is done by adding the markers which the body uses to recognise cells as 'self' and not part of an invading bacteria or virus, so that the immune system doesn't fight them—which would lead to rejection of the transplanted organ. Some concern has been expressed by the scientific community about the risk of virus transmission.

These concerns about the ethics and safety of xenotransplantation are being taken very seriously. However, the anti-vivisectionists' opposition is a lot more fundamental—though it is difficult to see why using pig products to save someone's life is worse than using them to make a bacon sandwich!

> "*The commercialization of science in genetic engineering biotechnology has compromised the integrity of scientists [and] reduced organisms, including human beings, to commodities.*"

Genetic Engineering Is Dangerous

Michael W. Fox

Michael W. Fox contends in the following viewpoint that genetic engineering threatens food safety, human health, animal welfare, and the environment. He claims that genetically engineering food plants can cause adverse immune-system reactions and allergies in the humans who eat them. In addition, genetically modified animals often suffer serious physical disabilities and could disrupt natural ecosystems if they escaped into the wild. Michael W. Fox is a senior scholar of bioethics for the Humane Society of the United States.

As you read, consider the following questions:

1. According to Fox, what percentage of all processed foods in the United States contain genetically engineered ingredients?
2. What is pleiotropism, according to the author?
3. According to the author, what is "terminator" gene technology?

If you are concerned about your health, animal suffering, environmental protection, and wildlife conservation, then you should be concerned about what genetic engineering is doing to animals, plants, and the environment. This new biotechnology industry, with its promises of medical progress and food for all, calls itself the "life science" industry. It is being vigorously promoted with minimal oversight and regulation by the U.S. government and other governments around the world, and the primary beneficiaries are investors and the multinational petrochemical/food and drug/industrial complex.

This new technology employs various ways to introduce genetic material from one species into another. Genes from fish, insects, bacteria, and viruses are put into the plants we eat, and some human genes are inserted into plants and nonhuman animals. These methods of "gene splicing" and the novel life forms so created are being patented and put on the market without clear scientific evidence that they are safe.

The History of Biotechnology

The development of the biotechnology industry took off in 1976 when Genentech Inc. in San Francisco became the first corporation formed to develop this technology. In 1980, the U.S. Supreme Court ruled that an oil-eating bacterium developed by a General Electric Company researcher for cleaning up oil spills could be patented. In this same year, scientists at Ohio University in Athens transferred human growth genes into mice to create the first transgenic animals. In 1982, the first genetically engineered (g.e.) pharmaceutical product (insulin) was approved by the U.S. Food and Drug Administration (FDA) for human use; g.e. rennin, an enzyme used to make cheese, was approved in 1990.

The U.S. Patent and Trademark office announced in 1987—against strong public opposition—that nonhuman animals are patentable subject matter, and in 1988 awarded the first patent to a g.e. cancer-prone mouse created at Harvard University. In 1990 the Bush administration set up the Competitiveness Council Biotechnology Working Group, headed by Vice President Dan Quayle, to essentially protect the emerging U.S. biotechnology industry from regulatory constraints in order to facilitate global market expansion. The Clinton administration was similarly pro-biotechnology, and ignored position papers and appeals by concerned scientists with the Environmental Protection Agency and FDA to proceed with caution because of potential adverse environmental and consumer health risks.

Today, some 60 percent of all processed foods in the United States contain g.e. ingredients; more than half of the soybean crop and a quarter of all corn is genetically engineered. The current market for g.e. seeds is estimated at $2.5 billion and involves four major industrial crops: soybeans, corn (maize), cotton, and canola (rapeseed). Argentina, Canada, and the United States grow the most g.e. crops, with China possibly in fourth place. Monsanto's patented g.e. seed traits accounted for more than four-fifths of the world's 1999 harvest of g.e. crops. The government refuses to require labeling of such foods to uphold the consumers' right to know.

The Frankenstein Factor

It has been established that pesticides and herbicides cause a variety of health and environmental problems that were long denied or covered up until Rachel Carson's book *Silent Spring* was published in 1962. These chemicals cannot self-replicate, but many genetically engineered organisms can. These organisms—containing new gene constructs (variously recombinant DNA) that have not been present in any life form ever before—can multiply and quickly spread these genes into the natural world. Today there are thousands of varieties of g.e. organisms, ranging from microbes to mice and tomatoes to trees, many of which are internationally patented. The risks that these g.e. organisms pose may well outweigh their hoped-for benefit.

Researchers have shown that recombinant DNA can pass from one organism and species to another, resulting in what I call "genetic pollution" of the life stream. Recombinant DNA—such as a novel construction of a virus in a g.e. crop—could combine with other viruses and mutate, causing new diseases in plants and animals, and have a half-life of maybe millions of years. Most g.e. crops contain so-called antibiotic "marker" genes, and many scientists fear that these could lead to even more widespread antibiotic resistance in bacteria that is already a serious public health concern, in part because of the use of antibiotics in livestock feed. This is because the marker genes carrying antibiotic resistance could be taken up by bacteria that would then become resistant to certain antibiotics.

RUNAWAY TRAIN

© Kirk Anderson. Reprinted with permission.

How can this technology have been allowed to develop so fast, and how can scientists, regulators, and other reasonable people ignore the law of unforeseen consequences and the precautionary principle? It was a combination of technology enchantment, arrogance and greed, coupled with an incomplete science-based understanding and socioeconomic assessment of risks and benefits, costs, and consequences. The precautionary principle (which employs both ethics and science in making risk assessments) and the law of unforeseeable consequences were ignored because biotechnology advocates believed they had the power to improve nature—and with patent protection for new products, they could create market monopolies and profit royally. But now things are beginning to fall apart, especially in the agricultural biotechnology sector.

Problems with Genetic Engineering

For example, pollen from genetically engineered crops has caused genetic contamination of conventional and organic crops that have had to be destroyed at great cost, along with contaminated food in the market.

The October 2000 recall of Taco Bell tortillas and a host of other products containing Aventis' g.e. corn—which the FDA has approved only for feeding to livestock because of possible allergic and other adverse immune-system reactions in humans—may cost Aventis close to $1.6 billion. But if the g.e. corn in these products was not considered safe for people, then what about residues from this feed in the milk, eggs, fat, and flesh of "pharm" animals fed such corn? Because of this logical connection between what livestock are fed and possible consumer risk from animal products, consumer groups in Britain are demanding that all such products be labeled to indicate whether or not the animals have been fed g.e. crops and related byproducts.

Thousands of varieties of transgenic mice have been created to serve as models for various human diseases so that new diagnostic procedures and therapeutic drugs can be developed. Critics lament that more animals than ever are being used in experiments that often cause much suffering and have more to do with profiting from, rather than preventing, disease. Mice with genetically engineered traits that lead to cancer, obesity, diabetes, and other disorders are regarded as high-fidelity models of analogous human diseases. But defective genes are not the sole cause of most human health problems, and from a more holistic medical perspective, the creation of these mouse "models" may not be as medically progressive as the advocates of transgenic mouse research claim. Now that scientists at the Oregon Regional Primate Research Center have created the first transgenic monkey, "ANDi" (who carries the fluorescence gene of a jellyfish), they hope to be able to soon produce monkeys with genes that cause Alzheimer's disease, breast cancer, hereditary blindness, and other ailments so new therapies and vaccines can be tested.

The U.S. government and the biotechnology industry have consistently demonstrated indifference toward animal suffering when preventing such suffering might reduce profits. For instance, when I and others testified against FDA approval of g.e. bovine growth hormone (rBGH), it was evident that injected cows would suffer more from production-related diseases because of hyperstimulation by the hormone, and have various health problems such as mastitis (udder infections), which could put consumers at risk. It was not clear that the milk from these cows that contained higher levels of insulin-like growth factor (which is elevated in people suffering from breast and prostate cancer) was safe for humans. But the FDA, bowing to industry pressure, approved this product and refused public appeals to have all dairy products from treated cows appropriately labeled.

Canada and several European countries banned rBGH because of the legitimate animal welfare and human health concerns. This resulted in a trade war with the United States, which called these other nations' responsible actions "protectionism" and which used the World Trade Organization (WTO) to force other countries to accept these products.

Pleiotropism

A major concern with genetically engineered organisms is the well-recognized problem called pleiotropism, the multiple and often unforeseen effects of a single gene. Genetic alteration to increase growth in pigs, or to confer insect and herbicide resistance in corn and cotton, can have unforeseen pleiotropic effects. As a consequence, biotechnologists have turned pigs into cripples with abnormal growth, defective joints, and impaired immune systems. The insertion of foreign genes can also cause mutations, which can mean birth defects and serious health problems later in life. There may also be so-called "overexpression" of the foreign genes so that excessive amounts of a particular hormone (like growth hormone) or other protein are produced. In animals, this may cause abnormal development and result in new diseases, difficult to diagnose and treat. In plants, insertional mutations and gene overexpression may result in new toxins harmful to consumers.

Although the cloning of plants occurs naturally through self-replication, the cloning of animals is unnatural and can result in a variety of problems including abortion, abnormal placentas, and often oversized fetuses with internal organ defects.

Scientists have created crops that are more susceptible to climatic extremes and produce far more insect poison than anticipated, which can actually leak through the roots and harm beneficial organisms in the soil and kill monarch butterflies and other harmless creatures. The g.e. insect poison called Bt (for Bacillus thuringiensis) may destroy soil mycorrhizal fungi. Without these fungi, which grow naturally around roots, plants cannot get essential nutrients from the soil, resulting in sick plants with poor nutritional value.

Few safety tests have been conducted on farmed animals fed transgenic crops. A . . . study by Steve Kestin and Toby Knowles at the University of Bristol found that the mortality rate of broiler chickens was doubled when the birds were fed Aventis corn that had been genetically engineered to be resistant to the toxic herbicide glufosinate ammonium and to produce the insecticidal Bt toxin Cry9c. . . .

Transgenic Animals

The creators of Dolly, the first cloned sheep, have . . . succeeded in cloning pigs. One genetically engineered line has been developed to serve as organ donors for humans. But this research has been stopped because of the legitimate fear that naturally occurring viruses in the pigs' organs could cause new plagues in the human population, with pig-organ recipients being potential disease time bombs. Yet in the United States and the United Kingdom, this research continues and entails much suffering for monkeys who are used as test recipients of g.e. pig hearts and kidneys.

While transgenic pigs are being produced to provide organs for humans, transgenic goats, sheep, chickens, cows, and pigs are being developed to produce new pharmaceutical products. Herds and flocks of such "pharm" animals will be established rapidly by cloning transgenic animals.

Salmon, catfish, and other "seafoods," as well as pigs, sheep, and cattle, are being genetically engineered to grow faster so human beings can eat ever more protein. The risks of transgenic fish escaping into rivers and seas and causing serious ecological disruptions of natural populations of aquatic life is one factor not to be ignored. Nor can the economic, ecological, and public health costs of increased animal protein and fat consumption be ignored, especially because there is a growing body of evidence supporting the savings and benefits of reduced meat production and consumption. Vegans and vegetarians should be aware of the environmental and ethical ramifications of g.e. crops that may well outweigh the health concerns, and buy organically certified produce.

The Gene Rush

The biotechnology industry is mounting a well-orchestrated public relations campaign to garner public trust and support. Universities, the government, and such prestigious institutions as the National Academy of Sciences and the Rockefeller Institute are endorsing agricultural biotechnology as the way to food security. They want the public to believe that g.e. food is safe and doesn't need to be labeled, and that this technology is the best, if not the only, way to feed the hungry world.

Critics see this as a cover by multinational corporations that are engaged in genetic piracy, which entails stealing the genetic resources—the so-called intellectual property—of peasant farmers' seed varieties, and even the unique DNA of indigenous peoples. There is a veritable gene rush going on to find and patent commercially valuable genes. This is coupled with a concerted move by multinational corporations to monopolize agriculture, food production, and worldwide marketing through international patent protection and the WTO. The U.S. government even shares a patent that will make all farmers' seeds sterile. This so-called "terminator" gene technology would prevent farmers from being able to save the best seeds for the next season, and instead force them to buy new seeds every year. Pollen from such "terminator" crops could sterilize conventional crops, valuable indigenous and traditional varieties, and wild plant relatives.

The U.S. government is aggressively seeking to force g.e. crops and food products on its own citizens and on foreign countries through its various State Department consular offices that encourage Third World governments to adopt

U.S. agricultural production methods and products, including g.e. seeds. So what's to be done with this runaway technology that impacts our food, our health, the well-being of animals and the environment? The gene genie is now way out of the bottle, and we can't put it back. Even if the release of g.e. life forms stopped tomorrow, we may not know for decades, if ever, their full impact on the life stream and future of Earth's creation.

As Mae-Wan Ho, Ph.D., with London's Open University, observes, "The commercialization of science in genetic engineering biotechnology has compromised the integrity of scientists [and] reduced organisms, including human beings, to commodities. . . . It results in a monolithic wasteland of genetic determinist mentality that is the beginning of the brave new world."[1]

The first meeting of the United Nations Food and Agriculture Organization's Ethics Panel, held in November 2000, concluded that g.e. crops are risky, that the patenting of genes and other genetic material will lead to unacceptable monopolies and to crop genetic erosion (loss of crop biodiversity), and that "terminator" technology is unethical.

My hope is that the potential risks and adverse consequences of this new industry, already with its millions of acres of genetically engineered crops, trees, and millions of genetically engineered animals, will make us wake up and be more responsive to the needs of the planet, and of the poor. It may also help us become more aware of the biological significance and purpose of other species, especially the animals and those life forms in the soil whom we cannot see with the naked eye and upon whose well-being our own species depends.

---

1. A reference to the novel with the same name by Aldous Huxley in which humans are bred in test tubes by the government. Each human is genetically engineered to fulfill a specific function in society.

"The introduction of cloning will open new avenues of animal exploitation and will streamline some old ones."

Cloning Harms Animals

Andrew Breslin

Andrew Breslin is the American Anti-Vivisection Society's outreach coordinator. In the following viewpoint, he argues that cloning will lead to the abuse of animals by animal researchers and the agricultural industry. Breslin contends that scientists will clone genetically identical animals for use in unscientific and cruel animal experiments. Moreover, he claims that scientists working for the agriculture industry will clone animals that produce more milk and meat simply as a means of improving profits.

As you read, consider the following questions:

1. What does Breslin claim is missing from the public debate about cloning?
2. According to the author, what industry will abuse animal cloning the most?
3. What happened to pigs that were genetically altered by the agriculture industry, according to Breslin?

D olly, the sheep who is the first clone produced from cells taken from an adult mammal, has set off controversy throughout the world, but most of the discussion has centered around the implications of human cloning.[1] There has been a conspicuous absence in the public debate regarding the fundamental change in the relationships between human beings and the rest of nature which has come, and is continuing to unfold, as a result of the new biotechnology.

Animal Exploitation

The introduction of cloning will open new avenues of animal exploitation and will streamline some old ones. Dolly was "created" in the interests of a company which seeks to develop animals as "bioreactors"[animals that are genetically altered so that they produce substances that humans need in their milk]. Cloning is also likely to lead to the mass production of transgenic animals of all kinds, including animals designed for xenotransplantation [transplanting the organs of one species into another], if that frightening practice is not halted. Altering DNA is a tricky, often hit-or-miss business. Now animals successfully "created" with altered DNA will be copied many times, as if they were mere documents and not living beings.

It is probable that even "normal" animals used in laboratories will be cloned in the near future. In the quest to eliminate every variable other than the obvious one of the differences between the animals under study and the human recipients of the therapies which may one day result, scientists will soon have legions of genetically identical animals upon whom to perform experiments. Ironically, the humans who will one day receive the resulting medications are likely to remain as genetically diverse as ever, making experiments on homogenous animals even further removed from the reality of human medicine.

Although animal experimentation is an enormous industry, it is eclipsed by the animal agriculture industry. The number of animals who suffer and die to satisfy humans' un-

1. Dolly was cloned in 1996 by Ian Wilmut, Keith Campbell, and their colleagues at Roslin Institute and the biotech company PPL.

natural eating habits is many times that of those who suffer in laboratories—in fact, for all other human purposes combined. Therefore, in sheer numbers, cloning is likely to have its most dramatic impact on the animal victims of this industry.

The large-scale factory farming of animals is evidence of our arrogance as a species, treating other animals as nothing more than machinery. Now we are redesigning the "machines" themselves for no other purpose than to increase the economic returns of the industry.

Cloning for Dollars

The airwaves and newsprint are replete with promises of cloned "low-fat" cows and pigs. The primary purpose behind the technology is clear: To make meat production more profitable.

Gary Francione, *Chicago Tribune*, March 7, 1997.

For decades, animal agriculture industries have pursued biotechnology as a means of increasing profits. At a recent conference on the genetic modification of "livestock," representatives of these industries listened excitedly to presentations by Ian Wilmut, one of Dolly's "creators."

The successful cloning from a cell of an adult mammal has encouraged the animal agriculture industries, who eagerly look forward to knocking out or adding specific genes to produce more profitable animals. In the past, such attempts at manipulation produced nothing but additional suffering. For example, the genetic manipulation of pigs to make them leaner resulted in animals which developed ulcers, lameness, and other physical problems. Selective breeding, a slower form of our genetic control of animals, has also resulted in severe physical problems for animals.

Ethical Implications

Not surprisingly, the animal industries have ignored the ethical implications of the new technologies, apparently seeing nothing but dollar signs, and considering any deeper appraisal a nuisance. This statement by Gary Webber of the National Cattleman's and Beef Association typifies this myopic viewpoint: "I see more and more consumer pressure for 'natural approaches' to production." The furor over cloning, he said, reveals "a widening gap between science and public understanding. I think we are going to have people screaming, 'stop this train for a while,' while society confronts the ethical and health issues of animal modification."

The context of Mr. Webber's statement makes it clear that he feels that confronting ethical and health issues is something he'd prefer we not do.

It is particularly disturbing to see the intense debate over the bioethical issues concerning cloning human beings but little discussion of what it means to manipulate the very structure of other species to serve as meat and milk machines. Dolly symbolizes everything that is wrong with our relationship with other animals, not only born to serve misguided human desires, but actually designed for no other purpose. In a display of extreme and sad irony, Ian Wilmut received a package from some well-meaning Canadian school children: It was filled with birthday cards for Dolly.

*"Cloning 'could offer the most realistic
option for [saving] many of our best-loved
and ecologically most significant wild
creatures.'"*

Cloning Can Help Humans and Animals

Ian Wilmut, Keith Campbell, and Colin Tudge

In 1996, scientists Ian Wilmut and Keith Campbell made
history by cloning a sheep—which they named Dolly—from
an adult ewe. Writer Colin Tudge collaborated with Wilmut
and Campbell to write a book about their experience called
The Second Creation: Dolly and the Age of Biological Control. In
the following viewpoint, the authors contend that scientists
can use cloning to produce more suitable laboratory animals
and more productive dairy cows, and to reproduce endangered species. The authors claim that cloning avoids the
problems associated with inbreeding, which frequently results in offspring plagued by genetic disorders.

As you read, consider the following questions:
1. According to the authors, what is homozygosity?
2. What is the difference in milk production between wild
   cows and the most productive domesticated Friesians,
   according to the authors?
3. According to the authors, why are species such as
   rhinoceroses and orangutans more at risk of extinction?

Tomorrow's biology, swollen with the new techniques and insights that will accrue from the science and technologies of cloning, now promises us a measure of control over life's processes that in practice will seem absolute. It would be dangerous ever to suppose that we can understand all of life's processes exhaustively: this would lead us into the Greek sin of hubris, with all the penalties that follow. Yet our descendants will find themselves with power that seems limited only by their imagination—that, plus the laws of physics and the rules of logic.

Prediction is a dangerous game, but it is one we should never stop trying to play. So let us look at what seems feasible in the light of current knowledge. . . .

Cloning for the Laboratory

Cloning laboratory animals may seem too obvious to be worth comment, but there is more to it than meets the eye. The central aim, of course, is to produce animals for experimentation that are genetically uniform, so that when scientists try out a particular drug or training method or other procedure, they know that any differences they perceive are due to the procedure and not to genetic differences between the animals. But there are various difficulties. Notably, the traditional way—and up to now the only way—to produce genetically uniform strains of, say, mice has been by inbreeding. Closely related individuals are mated, and their offspring are remated, until a population is produced that is all of a muchness.

But as everyone knows, such inbreeding is dangerous. It is for this reason that various genetic disorders, including porphyria and hemophilia, have bedeviled various royal houses in Europe. The problem lies with excess *homozygosity*. Every individual inherits one set of genes from one parent, and another set from the other parent. If the two parents are not closely related, then the two sets of genes will differ somewhat. You might, for example, inherit a gene for red hair from your mother, and a gene for dark hair from your father. Then you are said to be *heterozygous* for that particular gene for hair color. But if you inherited a gene for red hair from both parents, you would be homozygous for that hair color gene. The trouble begins when one of the genes in a matching pair is a deleterious mutant—for example, the one that produces cystic fibrosis (CF). If you inherit a cystic fibrosis mutant from one parent and a normal gene from the other, then you will not suffer from the disease; your heterozygosity saves you. But if you inherit the CF gene from both parents, you will be affected. Of course, only a minority of genes are as harmful as the CF mutant, but the principle applies broadly, and too much homozygosity leads to the general loss of fitness known as inbreeding depression.

So if you produce laboratory animals simply by inbreeding, then you will perforce produce a great deal of homozygosity, which is likely to lead to inbreeding depression. In fact *most* attempts to produce purebred strains of laboratory mice have failed. The strains that exist today are the minority that have survived inbreeding, fortunate beasts that happen, by chance, to lack a significant number of genes that are deleterious so that they avoid the kinds of effects we see in cystic fibrosis. We have to conclude, though, that laboratory mice are genetically peculiar because most animals simply cannot withstand such a high degree of homozygosity. Yet it happens, too, that inbreeding does not produce quite such uniformity as might be supposed. Sometimes there has proved to be a remarkable amount of genetic variation (implying heterozygosity) in laboratory strains that are supposed to be completely uniform.

On the other hand, it would sometimes be good to work with creatures that are more "natural": that is, are more heterozygous. Cloning helps here, as well. It not only offers a route to complete genetic uniformity—at least of the nuclear genes—but also makes it possible to produce strains that are uniform but *not* homozygous. In fact, a highly heterozygous wild mouse—or in principle a wild anything—could be cloned to produce as many genetic facsimiles as required. We are so used to thinking that genetic uniformity can be produced only by inbreeding that we tend to assume that uniformity must imply homozygosity. But consider, say, any one variety of domestic potato. Any particular King Edward or Maris Piper might well be highly heterozygous, but since it is multiplied by cloning (via tubers), each individual potato is genetically similar to all the others, and so the variety as a whole is uniform.

The advantages that may accrue from producing genetically identical laboratory animal strains *without* inbreeding could, as the decades pass, prove very helpful.

Replicating the Elite

Similar considerations—and more—apply to the cloning of farm livestock. On the one hand, farmers seek uniformity: they want to know how their animals are liable to perform under particular conditions, when they are liable to mature, and so on; and so, of course, do their markets. On the other hand, farmers also seek optimum performance, where "optimum" does not necessarily mean "maximum," although increasingly this is the case. Among, say, dairy cattle there is a huge difference between the yield of the milkiest cows, commonly called elite animals, and of the least endowed. A wild cow produces around 300 gallons of milk in a year to feed her solitary calf, while many modern [domesticated] Friesians produce 2,000 gallons and more. Of course, a modern farmer would have a herd of purebred Friesians, but even in one elite herd, there is commonly a twofold difference between the milkiest animals (2,000 gallons) and the average (around 1,000 gallons). In general, farmers seek to bring the average up to the level of the best. But such "improvements" (this is the technical term) take a very long time. The farmer normally improves his herd by impregnating his better cows by [artificial insemination] with semen from an elite bull. But only half the calves produced will be female, and each of them takes three years from conception to first lactation (a working year for her own gestation, then a year to mature, then another nine months to produce a calf as a prelude to lactation). In short, raising the standard of a herd even when the farmer has access to the world's best bulls is a slow business. In breeding time, the average animals are commonly considered to be ten years behind the elite.

There are further complications. Just as animals (and plants) suffer from inbreeding depression when they are too homozygous, they can also experience what Charles Darwin called hybrid vigor when they are outbred and thus highly heterozygous. Farmers of animals, like growers of potatoes, would in general like to combine overall uniformity with individual heterozygosity. In addition, farmers often seek to combine the qualities of different breeds, so that dairy farmers commonly cross Friesian dairy cows with beefy bulls (such as Herefords or Charolais) to produce calves that are good for beef (since only a minority of calves born in a dairy herd are needed as herd replacements). Among sheep farmers, juggling the options between uplands and lowlands, the crossing permutations can be quite bewildering.

Frozen Zoos

Cloning endangered species is controversial, but we assert that it has an important place in plans to manage species that are in danger of extinction. Some researchers have argued against it, maintaining that it would restrict an already dwindling amount of genetic diversity for those species. Not so. We advocate the establishment of a worldwide network of repositories to hold frozen tissue from all the individuals of an endangered species from which it is possible to collect samples. Those cells—like the sperm and eggs now being collected in "frozen zoos" by a variety of zoological parks—could serve as a genetic trust for reconstituting entire populations of a given species.

Robert P. Lanza, Betsy L. Dresser, and Philip Damiani, *Scientific American*, November 2000.

In all such instances where the need is to raise herd quality quickly, and/or to combine uniformity with heterozygosity, cloning has an obvious role. A dairy farmer might improve his herd significantly in ten years by purchasing sperm from an elite bull, but he might achieve the same improvement in one season by furnishing his cows with ready-made embryos that have been cloned from some elite animal. No wonder the Americans invested so much in this technology in the 1980s. Of course, ultrahigh performance does raise special issues of animal welfare—which alone must set limits on what can be done. On the other hand, cloning and embryo transfer could be of particular value in the Third World, where cattle are vital to the economy, where they are often multipurpose (cows might be required to pull carts as well as to provide calves and milk, though they may feed mainly on straw and must withstand tropical heat), and where breeding is particularly difficult because of the many contrasting qualities that are required in any one animal. Whether the economic "incentives" exist to take the new technologies into poor countries is another question.

Cloning for Conservation

Cloning could also be of immense, perhaps even critical, value in animal conservation. Many have doubted this. The critics point out, for example, that the task for conservationists is to maintain the maximum possible genetic diversity within each breeding population and point out, rightly, that cloning does not increase diversity. It merely replicates what is there already. This is precisely the point. Conservationists cannot *add* to the range of genes that currently exists. But they must strive to minimize the rate at which genetic diversity is lost. The great enemy is "genetic drift," the steady loss of genetic variation, generation by generation. When animals breed, each parent passes on only *half* of his or her genes to each offspring. If the animal has hundreds or millions of offspring, like a fly or a codfish, then there is a very good chance that each parent will indeed pass on all of its genes, which will be spread randomly among the many offspring. But an animal like a rhinoceros or an orangutan may have only about half a dozen offspring in a lifetime, so some of its genes are liable to remain uninherited. If the population of rhinos or orangs is large, then any one variant of any one gene is liable to be contained within many different individuals, so the breeding animals should pass on all the genes in the total gene pool. But if the breeding population is low—as it is bound to be if the animal is already rare—then the less common genes may well be contained within only one or a few individuals, and the individual containing the rarest genes may well finish its reproductive life without passing them on. Hence generational loss of variation.

Conservation biologists attempt to minimize loss by genetic drift by complicated breeding schemes intended to ensure that each individual that can breed does indeed mate (while avoiding inbreeding), but these schemes are expensive and difficult to organize. Yet it would be technically easy to take tissue samples (biopsies) from representative members of all the endangered species of mammals that now exist (about 200 at least are priorities), culture them, and then put the cultures in deep freeze. (If the biopsies were simply frozen without culturing them first, they would probably be damaged. Cultures are two-dimensional—one cell layer thick—while biopsies are three-dimensional blocks of tissue; it is hard to freeze a block uniformly.) If the samples were well chosen, they could contain virtually all the genes now present in existing species. In fifty years' time, when the technology that produced Dolly is well advanced and can be extended readily to other species, and when the species that are now endangered are on their last legs and have lost much of their present variation through genetic drift, cells from those frozen cell cultures could be made into Dolly-style embryos, and future creatures could give birth to offspring as diverse as those of today. Since the present-day breeding schemes are so difficult to run and organize (among other things, they require cooperation among people who tend to be highly individualistic), the Dolly technology could offer the most realistic option for many of our best-loved and ecologically most significant wild creatures.

|"*We now have the technology to save many
| . . . lives by using animal organ donors.*"

Using Animals as Organ Donors Will Save Human Lives

Susan E. Paris

Susan E. Paris maintains in the following viewpoint that using animals as organ donors is necessary because there are not enough human donors to meet the demand for organs. Paris contends that thousands of human lives can be saved by transplanting the healthy organs of animals into humans with kidney, liver, and other problems. She claims that health risks—such as the transference of disease—associated with transplanting the organs of one species into another are negligible. Susan E. Paris is president of Americans for Medical Progress, an organization that works to raise public awareness concerning the use of animals in research.

As you read, consider the following questions:

1. What is xenotransplantation, according to Paris?
2. According to Paris, how are pigs used to help people with defective heart valves?
3. What is zoonosis, according to the author?

Excerpted from "Animals to Human Transplants Are Vital," by Susan E. Paris, *Knight-Ridder/ Tribune News Service*, February 20, 1997. Copyright © 1997 by Tribune Media Services. Reprinted with permission.

D espite years of the best public service campaigns Madi-son Avenue can muster, human donors account for only 10 percent of the hearts, kidneys, livers and other organs needed for transplants.

Nearly 50 thousand Americans are on a waiting list for organs. This year, the wait will prove too long for some, and three thousand people will die.

Xenotransplantation

We now have the technology to save many of those lives by using animal organ donors. Yet animal rights activists are branding the field of animal-to-human transplants—xenotransplantation—as "Frankenstein science," and are vowing to do everything possible to derail it.

The use of animal organs and tissues has been a part of medicine for decades. For example, people with defective heart valves can have them replaced with valves from pigs. The polio vaccine our children receive is made with monkey kidney cells. Until a synthetic was developed, diabetics used insulin manufactured from cows and pigs. Experiments implanting fetal pig cells into the brains of Parkinson's disease patients and calf cells into the spinal cord of terminal cancer patients to relieve pain are now being conducted.

Actual transplantation of animal organs into human patients is a logical extension of this research, given today's advances in anti-rejection technology [that minimizes the risk that the body will reject transplanted organs]. Xenotransplantation holds promise for effective treatments for a wide range of diseases.

In submitting proposed guidelines for animal-to-human-transplants, Food and Drug Administration (FDA) Commissioner David Kessler acknowledged that the situation is a "tightrope." "We are balancing a real need for treatment against some very real risks," he cautioned.

Zoonosis

Caution is the byword of researchers who are working in the field.

Zoonosis, the transmission of animal diseases to humans, is a very real possibility in any animal-human interchange.

However, the FDA guidelines would so closely regulate the conditions under which animal-to-human transplants may be conducted as to make that risk negligible. The animal donors, specially bred and raised for the purpose, would be closely monitored. A xenotransplant patient would be far less likely than a farmer, an animal care worker or even a pet owner to contract a disease from an animal.

Safeguards

If xenotransplantation is attempted, the effort should take place only in an institution with well-trained staff who have long experience in organ transplantation and the management of engraftation, the prevention of organ rejection, and the prevention or control of graft versus host disease.

The transplant team must have requisite expertise that includes skilled surgeons, experts in infectious diseases, a veterinarian who is a diplomate of the American College of Veterinary Medicine, a transplant immunologist, an expert in nosocomial (hospital induced) infections, and clinical microbiologists. These experts must truly function as a team whose members have deep respect for one another.

Charles P. McCarthy, *Hastings Center Report*, November/December 1999.

It's natural that as researchers probe deeper in this developing area of scientific inquiry, we are concerned about what could go wrong. Animal rights groups, by painting scare scenarios of out-of-control diseases, are preying on our trepidation and hoping that our fears will halt scientific advancement.

Research is not without risk. Scientists are working to reduce those risks. But without courage—the courage of scientists, doctors and patients—no medical progress could be achieved.

Courage

There's the courage of the parents of Baby Fae, who in 1985 gave permission to doctors to implant a baboon heart into their newborn daughter born with a hopelessly underdeveloped heart. Baby Fae, her surgical and care teams and her family never contracted any animal viruses. The child lived 20 days and greatly increased scientists' understanding of xenotransplants and organ rejection.

There's the courage of Dr. Thomas Starzl, who heads the Transplantation Institute of the University of Pittsburgh and pioneered baboon-to-human liver transplants. His staunch advocacy of xenotransplantation has made him a prime target of the wrath of the animal rights movement.

There's the courage of Jeff Getty, who underwent a baboon bone marrow transplant in December 1995 in an attempt to bolster his immune system in its 15-year battle with HIV. His doctors could not tell him with certainty what would happen when the marrow was infused into his bloodstream. He could have immediately died from shock. The experiment was a success because Getty proved that the procedure is safe. In 1997, Getty is doing well, has not developed any baboon viruses and is feeling better than he has in years. Scientists will add to their knowledge as they monitor Getty, and as the procedure is performed on subsequent AIDS patients.

Animal rights activists who oppose the use of animal organs for transplants must be awfully confident that they and their loved ones will never be on a waiting list for a human organ transplant. How else to explain their attempts to sabotage such a promising field of research?

Reacting to the release of the FDA's proposed guidelines, Dan Mathews of the animal protection organization People for the Ethical Treatment of Animals (PETA) called xenotransplantation "cruel." The real cruelty is that scientists have given us the technology but opposition by groups such as PETA threaten to keep the benefits of animal organ transplants from reaching those in need.

"The risk of infection and onward transmission [of disease] is at present too great to justify [the transplantation of animal organs into humans]."

Using Animals as Organ Donors Puts Human Lives at Risk

Jonathan Hughes

Jonathan Hughes asserts in the following viewpoint that transplanting the organs of animals into humans is unsafe and unethical. According to Hughes, animal diseases could be passed along to the human recipient and then transmitted by the patient to the general population. While the organ recipient may well accept these risks, Hughes contends that such transplantation procedures would unfairly put other people in danger without their knowledge or consent. Jonathan Hughes is a lecturer in political thought in the department of government at the University of Manchester.

As you read, consider the following questions:
1. According to Hughes, how might the rate of organ rejection be reduced?
2. Why is it impossible to calculate the risk of an epidemic caused by animal-to-human transplants, according to the author?
3. According to Hughes, what precautions does the Nuffield report suggest in order to reduce the risks associated with animal-to-human transplants?

Excerpted from "Exnografting: Ethical Issues," by Jonathan Hughes, *Journal of Medical Ethics*, vol. 24, pp. 18–24, February 1998. Copyright © 1998 by the BMJ Publishing Group. Reprinted with permission.

The idea of using animals as a source of organs for transplant into humans [known as xenotransplantation] has been around for some time, but until now these procedures have been bedevilled by problems of immune system rejection: few patients have survived more than a few weeks and many have died in a matter of hours or less. Recently, however, there has been an upsurge of interest, resulting from technological developments that offer improved prospects for xenograft recipients. Better immunosuppressive drugs may help to reduce the rate of rejection, particularly with organs from closely related species such as baboons, and genetic modification of donor animals (particularly pigs) may improve their organs' compatibility with human recipients and hence reduce human immune system responses. . . .

In exploring [the ethical issues surrounding xenotransplantation] it will be argued that although the 1997 reports for the Nuffield Council on Bioethics and the Department of Health have made important contributions to this debate, both reach conclusions that are insufficiently cautious in the light of the problems that they address. . . .

Effects on Other Humans

The most important [ethical] issues here are the risk that diseases transmitted from animals to humans may prove infectious between humans, leading perhaps to new AIDS-type epidemics, and the costs that will be borne by other patients if resources are redirected from other areas of medical research and treatment to fund xenotransplantation. The fact that xenotransplantation carries risks not just for the xenograft recipient but for the population generally is important because it takes the ethics of xenotransplantation outside the realm of individual consent and into the realm of *justice*, raising questions about the extent to which it is permissible for an individual to impose risks on others for his own benefit.

The issue of reallocating resources is not specific to xenotransplantation, but raises the same problems as the introduction of any other new and experimental treatment—problems of predicting future costs and benefits and of ensuring effective and equitable use of resources. The question here is whether xenotransplantation would be a better or worse use of resources than the available alternatives.

More Serious Problem

The risk of transmitting infectious diseases to the wider population, however, is an altogether more serious problem. We do accept the imposition of some risks on others for our own benefit (for example when we drive cars). However, there are limits to what we regard as acceptable (it is not acceptable, for example, to drive when drunk), and it is therefore necessary to consider the nature of the risk imposed on the wider population by xenotransplantation procedures. The difficulty for proponents of xenotransplantation is that the worst-case scenario (a major new epidemic) is extremely grave, and its likelihood is difficult if not impossible to quantify. As the Nuffield report explains:

> It will be very difficult to identify organisms that do not cause any symptoms in the animal from which they come. Previous experience indicates that infectious organisms are normally identified only after the emergence of the disease they cause. ... Put bluntly, it may be possible to identify any infectious organism transmitted by xenografting only if it causes disease in human beings, and after it has started to do so.

Moreover, if, as in the case of HIV, there is a long incubation period between infection and development of the disease, the agent may have spread far beyond the original xenograft recipient by the time its symptoms are noticed, undermining any hope of containing the infection. The Nuffield report concludes from these considerations that the risk of a major epidemic is unquantifiable, and in the light of this advocates a *precautionary principle*, requiring "that action should be taken to avoid risks *in advance* of certainty about their nature" and that "the burden of proof should lie with those developing the technology to demonstrate that it will not cause serious harm". Unfortunately, the measures that the report proposes in order to safeguard against disease transmission do not live up to this principle.

The report begins robustly enough, by stating:

> that the risks associated with possible transmission of infectious diseases as a consequence of xenotransplantation have not been adequately dealt with. It would not be ethical,

therefore to begin clinical trials of xenotransplantation involving human beings.

Insufficient Precautions

However, the report goes on to suggest that xenotransplantation should be allowed to proceed once the following conditions have been satisfied: (1) that "as much information as possible" be assembled about the risks of transmission; (2) that source animals be "reared in conditions in which all known infectious organisms are monitored and controlled"; (3) that early recipients undergo regular monitoring and testing; and (4) that there be "a commitment to suspend, modify or, if necessary, discontinue xenotransplantation procedures at any signs that new infectious diseases are emerging". These precautions, however, are far from watertight, for, as noted above, the report acknowledges that *full* knowledge of potentially ineffective agents is for all practical purposes impossible. A consequence of this is that source animals cannot be freed from *all* infectious organisms but only those that are known and can be reliably tested for: "Specified pathogen-free animals may still be infected with unidentified infectious organisms about which nothing is known". Because the risk of disease transmission cannot be eliminated, the report recommends that procedures for monitoring of recipients be established and that consent to this be included in consent to the xenograft. Monitoring, however, is of no use unless backed-up by a plan of action, and as the following passage demonstrates, the report fails utterly to provide such a plan.

> The most difficult question is what procedure should be followed if it is found that a disease has indeed been transmitted from the animals used to provide organs or tissue to human xenograft recipients? In principle, steps should be taken to prevent transmission of the disease to other people. In practice, this is a very difficult issue. For a start, it is very unlikely that, at the outset, the mode of transmission of the disease will be understood. The appropriate response will depend on the mode of transmission and on how infectious the disease is. It would hardly be acceptable to isolate xenograft recipients suffering from an infectious disease, or to ask them to refrain from sexual intercourse or, in the case of a virus transmitted from parent to offspring, from having children. This

highlights how difficult it would be to prevent the transmission of an infectious disease originating from xenotransplantation. It is sobering to reflect on the difficulty, despite globally coordinated attempts, of controlling and eliminating infectious diseases such as malaria, hepatitis and AIDS.

This is indeed a sobering passage, and given such pessimism about the prospects for containment of any new infection, the precautionary principle would appear to require that the proposed moratorium on xenotransplantation procedures be made indefinite.

Gamble. © 2000 the Florida Times-Union.

The Department of Health report goes further than the Nuffield report in discriminating the risks posed by different kinds of infectious agents, but reaches similar conclusions. Fungi, parasites and bacteria, it concludes, pose relatively little risk either to the xenograft recipient or to the wider population. With regard to prions, it holds that transmission to xenograft recipients is unlikely (though recent controversy about the transmissibility of prion disease from BSE-infected cattle [cattle with bovine spongiform encephalopathy, a fatal disease commonly called mad cow disease] to humans might lead us to doubt the reliability of scientific advice on this matter), and that prions are unlikely to be transmitted from one human to another. In view of the latter, the long incubation period typical of prion disease appears as an advantage rather than a disadvantage, allowing that even an infected recipient may benefit from years of good quality life, without posing a risk to others. The greatest risk, the report concludes, is from viruses, due to their transmissibility between humans, the long incubation periods of some viral infections, and our limited ability to screen for and exclude known and unknown viruses in donor animals. As far as viruses are concerned, the Department of Health report concurs with the Nuffield report that the risk of infection and onward transmission is at present too great to justify experimental procedures.

Future Acceptability

Unfortunately the Department of Health report runs into the same difficulties as the Nuffield report in considering the future conditions under which xenografting might become acceptable. It too premises the future acceptability of xenotransplantation upon the hope that further research may show the risk of infection to be "within tolerable margins", while acknowledging that it cannot ever be totally ruled out. In expressing this hope, however, the report ignores the difficulty, raised by the Nuffield report, of quantifying, and assessing as tolerable, a risk posed by agents that are as yet unidentified. The Department of Health report also follows the Nuffield report in advocating monitoring of xenograft recipients as a further safeguard against the spreading of infections and, again, like the Nuffield report, offers no satisfactory account of what should be done in the event of a positive result, suggesting only that "appropriate additional research" may be indicated. . . .

A moratorium should be imposed upon xenotransplantation procedures at least until possible avenues for increasing the supply of human organs have been exhausted and until a more reassuring judgment can be reached on the prospects for preventing and containing transmitted infections.

Periodical Bibliography

The following articles have been selected to supplement the diverse views presented in this chapter. Addresses are provided for periodicals not indexed in the *Readers' Guide to Periodical Literature*, the *Alternative Press Index*, the *Social Sciences Index*, or the *Index to Legal Periodicals and Books*.

Lawrence Carter-Long	"Current Pig Research," *Mainstream*, Fall 1997.
Joseph F. Coates, John B. Mahaffie, and Andy Hines	"The Promise of Genetics," *Futurist*, September/October 1997.
Steven Alan Edwards	"Pork Liver Anyone?" *Technology Review*, July 1996.
Gary Francione	"Cloning Breeds Contempt and Adulation," *Chicago Tribune*, March 7, 1997.
Robert P. Lanza, Betsy Dresser, and Philip Damiani	"Cloning Noah's Ark," *Scientific American*, November 1, 2000.
Mark Nichols	"Organs on Demand: The Cloning of Pigs Is a Step Towards Producing Spare Parts for Humans," *Maclean's*, August 8, 2000.
Joni Praded	"The Next Frontier: Animals 2000," *Animals*, September/October 1998.
Andrew Ross	"An Interview with Ian Wilmut: Dr. Frankenstein, I Presume," *Salon*, February 24, 1997, www.salonmagazine.com.
William H. Velander et al.	"Transgenic Livestock as Drug Factories," *Scientific American*, January 1, 1997.
Bruce Wallace	"The Dolly Debate: A Sheep Cloned in Scotland Raises Hopes and Fears About a Fantastic Technology," *Maclean's*, March 10, 1997.
Susan Wright	"Down on the Animal Pharm," *Nation*, March 11, 1996.

For Further Discussion

Chapter 1

1. Tom Regan argues that giving animals rights would help society become more compassionate. On the other hand, Charles R. Pulver contends that God gave humans authority over the animals and encouraged them to use animals as they saw fit. Do you think that kindness toward animals can help develop compassion for other people? Please explain your answer.

2. The Animal Liberation organization contends that animals and humans are morally equal. In contrast, Damon Linker maintains that animals cannot reason morally and are therefore inferior to humans. Do you agree with Linker that animals do not know right from wrong? In constructing your argument, provide specific examples of animal behavior with which you are familiar. Make sure to make clear the distinction between *instinct* and *reasoning*.

3. Norm Phelps cites portions of the core ethical teachings of some of the world's major religions to support his argument that religion can be used to advance animal rights. Conversely, Seriously Ill for Medical Research supplies quotes from prominent figures within major religious organizations to support its argument that religion does not support equal rights for animals. In your opinion, which argument is more convincing? Please cite specifics from each text while constructing your answer.

4. Cal Thomas argues that animal rights activists are terrorists because they use violence to help further their cause. Jane Cartmill disagrees with Thomas, claiming that activists do not use violence. Describe activities that you think animal rights activists could engage in that would be both effective and morally acceptable.

Chapter 2

1. Robert Garner contends that it is unethical to use animals for research because they have the same moral value as humans. Conversely, Henry E. Heffner argues that it is ethical to use animals for research because they actually fare better in the laboratory environment than they would in their natural habitats. Suppose that Heffner is correct that lab animals breed more successfully than their wild counterparts, do you think that it is right for people to make such decisions about the fates of other creatures? Please explain your answer.

2. Jack H. Botting and Adrian R. Morrison use several examples of medical breakthroughs to support their argument that animal

testing is vital to medicine. C. Ray Greek and Jean Swingle Greek cite cases where medical experiments on animals failed in order to support their argument that animal experimentation is unscientific. Which pair of authors do you think uses examples most convincingly? Cite several of the specific examples the authors use while developing your answer.

Chapter 3

1. In Defense of Animals argues that the committees charged with overseeing the welfare of laboratory animals are ineffective because their members consist of scientists who are sympathetic to biomedical research and of people in the community who are easily manipulated. However, Delmas Luedke—who works at a medical center and once served on an animal welfare committee—contends that such committees succeed in protecting the welfare of animals used in biomedical experiments. In your opinion, do Luedke's credentials bolster or hurt his argument? Please explain.

2. The Southwest Foundation for Biomedical Research claims that because nonhuman primates are so physically similar to humans they are essential research models in studying human diseases. In contrast, the Coalition to End Primate Experimentation asserts that because nonhuman primates are so similar to people they are morally equal to humans and cannot ethically be experimented on. In your opinion, does the fact that apes and humans are so similar support the view that apes should be used in animal experimentation or does it bolster the argument that doing so would be immoral? Please explain your answer.

3. Animal Aid contends that dogs should not be used for medical experiments while the Foundation for Biomedical Research argues that dogs are essential research models in the study of human diseases. Do you think companion animals such as dogs and cats should be given greater ethical consideration than other animals typically used in research such as mice and rabbits? That is, do you think pets have a higher moral worth than other animals? Please explain.

4. F. Barbara Orlans maintains that mice and rats should be included in the Animal Welfare Act because they feel pain in the same way that animals included in the Act do. On the other hand, Debra J. Saunders claims that including rats and mice in the Act will hinder medical research. Would you be in favor of extra protections for laboratory animals such as mice even if new laws slowed the progress of medical research into human dis-

eases? When formulating your answer, justify your position as specifically as you can.

Chapter 4

1. Michael W. Fox argues that genetic engineering has developed so fast without adequate regulation that it threatens the health of humans and animals. However, Kevin O'Donnell contends that genetic engineering has been benefiting people since humans first domesticated animals thousands of years ago. Does the speed of progress in and the degree of oversight over the field of genetic engineering concern you? In formulating your answer, discuss your reactions to specific advances in biotechnology such as cloning and xenotransplantation.

2. Andrew Breslin asserts that scientists who are cloning animals—most of whom he claims work for the food industry—are motivated solely by profit and are unconcerned about human and animal welfare. Ian Wilmut, Keith Campbell, and Colin Tudge agree that cloned animals will be used to increase food industry profits, but they still see cloning as beneficial. In your opinion, does the fact that scientists might be financially rewarded for their achievements undermine the validity and potential benefit of their work? While formulating your answer, consider what motivates scientists—money, prestige, curiosity, compassion—and decide which inducements you think can produce the most beneficial science.

3. Susan E. Paris supports her argument that animals should be used as organ donors by citing specific scientists, doctors, and patients who took risks that have advanced the field of xenotransplantation. Jonathan Hughes argues that transplanting the organs of animals into humans is too risky and supports his contention by citing studies that outline the specific risks of disease associated with such procedures. In your opinion, which author's use of evidence is more convincing? Please explain your answer.

Organizations to Contact

The editor has compiled the following list of organizations concerned with the issues debated in this book. The descriptions are derived from materials provided by the organizations. All have publications or information available for interested readers. The list was compiled on the date of publication of the present volume; names, addresses, phone and fax numbers, and e-mail and Internet addresses may change. Be aware that many organizations take several weeks or longer to respond to inquiries, so allow as much time as possible.

American Anti-Vivisection Society (AAVS)
801 Old York Rd., Suite 204, Jenkintown, PA 19046
(215) 887-0816 • fax: (215) 887-2088
website: www.aavs.org

AAVS advocates the abolition of vivisection, opposes all types of experiments on living animals, and sponsors research on alternatives to these methods. The society produces videos and publishes numerous brochures, including *Vivisection and Dissection and the Classroom: A Guide to Conscientious Objection* and the bimonthly *AV Magazine*.

American Association for Laboratory Animal Science (AALAS)
9190 Crestwyn Hills Dr., Memphis, TN 38125
(901) 754-8620 • fax: (901) 759-5849
website: www.aalas.org

AALAS is a professional nonprofit association concerned with the production, care, and study of animals used in biomedical research. The association provides a medium for the exchange of scientific information on all phases of laboratory animal care and use through educational activities, publications, and certification program.

Americans for Medical Progress (AMP)
421 King St., Suite 401, Alexandria, VA 22314
(703) 836-9595 • fax: (703) 836-9594
e-mail: info@amprogress.org • website: www.amprogress.org

AMP is a nonprofit organization working to raise public awareness concerning the use of animals in research in order to ensure that scientists and doctors have the freedom and resources necessary to pursue their research. AMP exposes the misinformation of the animal rights movement through newspaper and magazine articles, broadcast debates, and public education materials.

Animal Aid
The Old Chapel, Bradford St., Tonbridge, Kent, TN9 1AW, United Kingdom
44 (0) 1732 364546 • fax: 44 (0) 1732 366533
e-mail: info@animalaid.org.uk • website: www.animalaid.org.uk

Animal Aid investigates and exposes animal cruelty. The organization stages street protests and education tours, and publishes educational packs for schools and colleges.

Animal Alliance of Canada
221 Broadway Ave., Suite 101, Toronto, ON, M4M 2G3, Canada
(416) 462-9541 • fax: (416) 462-9647
website: www.animalalliance.ca

The Animal Alliance of Canada is an animal rights advocacy and education group that focuses on local, regional, national, and international issues concerning the good will toward and respectful treatment of animals by humans. The alliance acts through research, investigation, education, advocacy, and legislation. Publications include fact sheets, legislative updates, editorials, and the newsletter *TakeAction*.

Animal Welfare Institute (AWI)
PO Box 3650, Washington, DC 20007
(202) 337-2332 • fax: (202) 338-9478
e-mail: awi@animalwelfare.org • website: www.animalwelfare.org

Founded in 1951, the AWI is a nonprofit charitable organization working to reduce pain and fear inflicted on animals by humans. AWI believes in the humane treatment of laboratory animals and the development and use of nonanimal testing methods, and encourages humane science teaching and prevention of painful experiments on animals by high school students. In addition to publishing *AWI Quarterly*, the institute also offers numerous books, pamphlets, and online articles.

Coalition to End Primate Experimentation (CEPE)
54 Gray Lawn, Petaluma, CA 94952
e-mail: cepemail@yahoo.com • website: http://cepe.enviroweb.org

CEPE is a loosely organized group of activists with a common desire to see harmful experimentation on nonhuman primates ended at once. The group is organized specifically to target the eight federally-funded "Regional Primate Research Centers" that conduct biomedical experiments on nonhuman primates throughout the United States.

Fund for Animals

200 West 57th St., New York, NY 10019

(212) 246-2096 • fax: (212) 246-2633

e-mail: fundinfo@fund.org • website: www.fund.org

The Fund for Animals was founded in 1967 by prominent author and animal advocate Cleveland Armory. It is one of the largest and most active organizations working for the welfare of both wild and domestic animals throughout the world. The fund works on education, legislation, litigation, and hands-on animal care.

Incurably Ill for Animal Research

PO Box 27454, Lansing, MI 48909

(517) 887-1141

e-mail: info@iifor.org • website: www.iifor.org

This organization consists of people who have incurable diseases and are concerned that the use of animals in medical research will be stopped or severely limited by animal rights activists, thus delaying or preventing the development of new cures. It publishes the monthly *Bulletin* and a quarterly newsletter.

In Defense of Animals

131 Camino Alto, Suite E, Mill Valley, CA 94941

(415) 388-9641 • fax: (415) 388-0388

e-mail: ida@idausa.org • website: www.idausa.org

In Defense of Animals is a nonprofit organization established in 1983 that works to end the institutional exploitation and abuse of laboratory animals. The organization publishes fact sheets and brochures on animal abuse in the laboratory and on how to live a cruelty-free lifestyle.

Institute for In Vitro Sciences

21 Firstfield Rd., Suite 220, Gaithersburg, MD 20878

(301) 947-6523 • fax: (301) 947-6538

website: www.iivs.org

The institute is a nonprofit technology-driven foundation for the advancement of alternative methods to animal testing. Its mission is to facilitate the replacement of animal testing through the use of in vitro technology, conduct in vitro testing for industry and government, and provide educational and technical resources to public and private sectors.

Medical Research Modernization Committee (MRMC)
20145 Van Aken Blvd., Suite 24, Shaker Heights, OH 44122
(216) 283-6702
website: www.mrmcmed.org

MRMC is a national health advocacy group composed of physicians, scientists, and other health care professionals who evaluate the benefits, risks, and costs of medical research methods and technologies. The committee believes that animals are inadequate models for testing medical treatments and that research money would be better spent on human clinical research studies.

National Animal Interest Alliance (NAIA)
PO Box 66579, Portland, OR 97290
(503) 761-1139
e-mail: NAIA@naiaonline.org • website: www.naiaonline.org

NAIA is an association of business, agricultural, scientific, and recreational interests formed to protect and promote humane practices and relationships between people and animals. NAIA provides the network necessary for diverse animal rights groups to communicate with one another, to describe the nature and value of their work, to clarify animal rights misinformation, and to educate each other and the public about what they do. NAIA serves as a clearinghouse for information and as an access point for subject matter experts, keynote speakers, and issue analysts. The alliance also publishes the bimonthly newspaper *NAIA News*.

The Nature of Wellness
PO Box 10400, Glendale, CA 91209
(818) 790-6384 • fax: (818) 790-9660
website: www.animalresearch.org

The Nature of Wellness is a nonprofit organization whose objective is to bring about total abolition of the practice of animal experimentation. The Nature of Wellness informs the public about the medical and scientific invalidity and counterproductiveness of animal experimentation and the massive damage it causes to human health, the environment, and the economy through print ads and its television documentary *Lethal Medicine*.

People for the Ethical Treatment of Animals (PETA)
501 Front St., Norfolk, VA 23510
(757) 622-7382 • fax: (757) 622-0457
e-mail: peta@norfolk.infini.net • website: www.peta.org

An international animal rights organization, PETA is dedicated to establishing and protecting the rights of all animals. It focuses on four areas: factory farms, research laboratories, the fur trade, and the entertainment industry. PETA promotes public education, cruelty investigations, animal rescue, celebrity involvement, and legislative action. It produces numerous videos and publishes *Animal Times, Grrr!*, various fact sheets, brochures, and flyers.

Physicians Committee for Responsible Medicine (PCRM)
5100 Wisconsin Ave., Suite 404, Washington, DC 20016
(202) 686-2210 • fax: (202) 686-2216
e-mail: pcrm@pcrm.org • website: www.pcrm.org
Founded in 1985, PCRM is a nonprofit organization supported by physicians and laypersons to encourage higher standards for ethics and effectiveness in research. It promotes using nonanimal alternatives in both research and education. The committee publishes the quarterly magazine *Good Medicine* and numerous fact sheets on animal experimentation issues.

Psychologists for the Ethical Treatment of Animals (PSYETA)
403 McCauley St., PO Box 1297, Washington Grove, MD 20880
(301) 565-4167
website: www.psyeta.org
PSYETA seeks to ensure proper treatment of animals used in psychological research and education and urges revision of curricula to include ethical issues in the treatment of animals. It developed a tool to measure the invasiveness or severity of animal experiments. Its publications include the book *Animal Models of Human Psychology* and the journals *Society and Animals* and *Journal of Applied Animal Welfare Science*.

Regional Primate Research Centers
National Institute of Health
website: www.ncrr.nih/gov/compmed/cmrprc.htm
Regional Primate Research Centers are a national network of eight centers that provide specialized facilities for nonhuman primate research, highly experienced personnel, and appropriate research environments. These support the development of nonhuman primate models and research resources for studies of critical importance for understanding human health problems and disease processes. Collectively, the eight centers assist more than one thousand scientists who use nonhuman primates as the most appropriate animal models for studies of AIDS, cancer, Alzheimer's disease, Parkinson's disease, leprosy, and cardiovascular diseases.

Seriously Ill for Medical Research
PO Box 504, Dunstable, Bedfordshire, LU6 2LU, United
Kingdom
(44) 01582 873108 • fax: (44) 01582 873705
e-mail: SIMR@dircon.co.uk • website: www.simr.org.uk

SIMR is a patients' group formed to voice support for humane research into disabling, incurable, and progressive diseases. SIMR
promotes the following objectives: a greater public understanding
of the methods, aims, and benefits of animal research; the provision of the resources necessary for medical research to be conducted; and appropriate legislation relating to medicine and medical research. The group publishes a quarterly newsletter and an
annual report.

Bibliography of Books

Robert. M. Baird and Stuart E. Rosenbaum, eds.	*Animal Experimentation: The Moral Issues.* New York: Prometheus Books, 1998.
Baruch A. Brody	*The Ethics of Biomedical Research.* New York: Oxford University Press, 1998.
Stephen Budiansky	*If a Lion Could Talk: Animal Minds and the Evolution of Consciousness.* New York: Free Press, 1998.
Stephen R.L. Clark	*Animals and Their Moral Standing.* New York: Routledge, 1997.
Pietro Croce	*Vivisection or Science? An Investigation into Testing Drugs and Safeguarding Health.* New York: Zed Books, 1999.
Nancy Day	*Animal Experimentation: Cruelty or Science?* Springfield, NJ: Enslow, 2000.
David DeGrazia	*Taking Animals Seriously: Mental Life and Moral Status.* New York: Cambridge University Press, 1998.
Kevin Dolan	*Ethics, Animals, and Science.* Malden, MA: Blackwell Science, 1999.
Alix Fano	*Lethal Laws: Animal Testing, Human Health, and Environmental Policy.* New York: Zed Books, 1997.
Michael Allen Fox	*The Case for Animal Experimentation: An Evolutionary and Ethical Perspective.* Berkeley: University of California Press, 1986.
Robert Garner	*Political Animals: Animal Protection Politics in Britain and the United States.* New York: St. Martin's, 1998.
C. Ray Greek and Jean Swingle Greek	*Sacred Cows and Golden Geese: The Human Cost of Experiments on Animals.* New York: Continuum, 2000.
Julian McAllister Groves	*Hearts and Minds: The Controversy over Lab Animals.* Philadelphia: Temple University Press, 1997.
Harold D. Guither	*Animal Rights: History and Scope of a Radical Social Movement.* Carbondale: Southern Illinois University Press, 1998.
Lynette A. Hart, ed.	*Responsible Conduct with Animals in Research.* New York: Oxford University Press, 1998.
Chris Hayhurst	*Animal Testing: The Animal Rights Debate.* New York: Rosen, 2000.

Vaughan Monamy	*Animal Experimentation: A Guide to the Issues.* New York: Cambridge University Press, 2000.
Daniel T. Oliver and Robert Huberty, eds.	*Animal Rights: The Inhumane Crusade.* New York: Merril, 1999.
F. Barbara Orlans et al.	*The Human Use of Animals: Case Studies in Ethical Choice.* New York: Oxford University Press, 1998.
Ellen Frankel Paul et at.	*Why Animal Experimentation Matters: The Use of Animals in Medical Research.* Washington, DC: Social Philosophy Policy Center, 2001.
Tom Regan	*The Case for Animal Rights.* Berkeley: University of California Press, 1983.
Bernard E. Rollin	*The Frankenstein Syndrome: Ethical Social Issues in the Genetic Engineering of Animals.* New York: Cambridge University Press, 1995.
Deborah Rudacille	*The Scalpel and the Butterfly: The War Between Animal Research and Animal Protection.* New York: Farrar, Straus and Giroux, 2000.
Brian C. Shaefer, ed.	*Gene Cloning and Analysis: Current Innovations.* Portland, OR: Horizon Scientific, 1997.
Kenneth Joel Shapiro	*Animal Models of Human Psychology: Critique of Science, Ethics, and Policy.* New York: Hogrefe and Huber, 1997.
Peter Singer	*Ethics into Action: Henry Spira and the Animal Rights Movement.* New York: Rowman and Littlefield, 1998.
Peter Singer, ed.	*In Defense of Animals.* New York: Blackwell, 1985.
Stephen Webb	*On God and Dogs: A Christian Theology of Compassion for Animals.* New York: Oxford University Press, 1998.
Ian Wilmut, Keith Campbell, and Colin Tudge	*The Second Creation: Dolly and the Age of Biological Control.* New York: Farrar, Straus and Giroux, 2000.
Stephen Wise	*Rattling the Cage: Toward Legal Rights for Animals.* Cambridge: Perseus Books, 2000.

Index

testing with animals, 15

endangered species, 27–28, 173–74
Endangered Species Act (1973), 28
Epstein, Richard A., 38

farm animals. *See* animals
farming, 165–66
Fauci, Anthony S., 113
Finland, 137
fish, 161–62
Fishbein, Estelle, 42, 140
Fleming, Alexander, 81–82
Florey, Howard W., 82
Food and Drug Administration (FDA), 177
food, 157–58
Foundation for Biomedical Research, 127
Fox, Michael W., 155
Francione, Gary, 166
Freeh, Louis, 58

Galen, 14
Garner, Robert, 68
Genentech Inc., 156
gene therapy
  and cloning, 149–50
  first attempts at, 152
  types of, 150
  and use of transgenic animals, 151–52
  using good genes for, 150–51
genetic code, 148
genetic engineering
  and DNA, 147–49
  of food crops, 157–58
  and genetic piracy, 162–63
  government indifference toward, 159–60
  history of, 156–57
  old and new methods in, 147
  and patents, 162
  problems with, 159, 160–61
  see also cloning; gene therapy
genocide, 31
germ-line therapy, 150
Getty, Jeff, 178
Ghoniem, Gamal M., 119
Gibbon, John, 82
Glaxo-Wellcome, 123
God, 28, 47
Goodall, Jane, 32, 40, 116
Graham, Jennifer, 67
Greek, C. Ray, 87
Greek, Jean Swingle, 87
guinea pigs, 84, 108

hamsters, 108
Heffner, Henry E., 72
heparin, 83
herbicides, 157
Hinduism, 55
Hippocrates, 14
Ho, Mae-Wan, 163
Howell, Leonard L., 119–20
Hughes, Jonathan, 179
Human Genome Project, 149
humans
  animal suffering permitted for
    benefit of, 69
  animals benefit from relationship
    with, 73–75
  are not superior to animals, 21
  cloning genes of, into animals,
    152–53
  as differing from animals, 40–41,
    88–89
  dominion over all living things, 28
  lack of physiological differences
    between animals and, 83–84
  parallels between animals and, 39–40
  religions valuing over animal life, 51
  rights of
    declaration of, 30
    and duties, 26
    and genocide, 31
    and slavery, 30–31
  sacrificing the few for the many,
    76–77
  similarities with primates, 116–18
  used in medical research, 102, 108
  see also animals, as organ donors
Human Society of the U.S. (HSUS),
    58
Huntingdon Life Sciences (HLS), 124

inbreeding, 169–71, 173–74
In Defense of Animals, 99, 101–102
infectious diseases, 79–80, 82
Institute of Psychiatry, 123
Institutional Animal Care and Use
  Committees, 16, 103
  oversight by, 107–108
Islam, 55
isomorphism, 89–90

Jainism, 47, 48
Johns Hopkins University, 140
Jones, Steve, 145
Judaism, 54

Kessler, David, 176
Kestin, Steve, 161
kidneys, 82–83
Kinsey, Janice H., 118

gaining moral values from, 51
God's sentiments on animal rights, 28
reasons to engage animal rights
movement with, 45–47
supporting animal rights, 47
reproduction, animal, 73–74, 75
research
agricultural, 98
for profit, 166
suffering in, vs. animals suffering in
labs, 165–66
on animals
and change in lifestyle, 84
cloning animals for, 169–71
committee reviewing
low reliability of, 103–105
oversight by, 107–108
debate on, 16–17, 107
developing transgenic animals for,
151–52
dissection, 67
financing, 94, 100
history of, 14–15, 73
increased lifespans from, 82
and laboratory environment, vs.
wild habitat, 75–76
lack of oversight on, 100, 102–103,
104–105
as minimizing total suffering,
108–109
misleading and dangerous data
from, 91–92
moral case against, 69–70
public opinion on, 14, 16
reasons for continued, 94–95
reducing, 70–71, 137
does not benefit animals, 74–75
religions on, 47, 52–56
as a "sacred cow," 88
and sacrificing the few for the
many, 76–77
safety and effectiveness of medical
advances from, 90–91
scientific doubters on, 93–94
types of animals used in, 111
violates animal rights, 32–33
violence in, 62–64
as vital to medical progress, 79–83,
84–86, 111, 113
con, 89, 92–93
whistleblowers exposing
wrongdoing in, 105
heart, 125–26, 128
see also Animal Welfare Act;
individual animals
Roberts, William Clifford, 125–26
rodents, 83, 101
Ronnekleiv, Oline K., 118

Rulf-Fountain, Alyssa, 118, 119
Russell, George, 67
Russell, William, 15

Sacred Cows and Golden Fleece: The
Human Cost of Experiments on Animals
(Greek and Greek), 87, 94
Saunders, Debra J., 139
Schwambach, Stephen, 19
Science (journal), 103–104
Scruton, Roger, 27
Seriously Ill for Medical Research
(SIMR), 50
Sikhism, 55
Silent Spring (Carson), 157
Singer, Peter, 16, 33, 34, 40–41, 42
slavery, 30–31
Smith, Beth, 53
SmithKline Beecham, 123
Southwest Foundation for Biomedical
Research, 110
Soviet Union, 116
speciesism, 21, 33–34, 38, 69
Starzl, Thomas, 178
suffering
and animal rights, 22
vs. inflicting, 37–39
of animals, for benefit of humans, 69
sulfonamides, 81
surgery, 82
Switzerland, 137

thalidomide, 83–84
Thomas, Cal, 57, 62, 64
Tigges, Margarete, 120
transplants, organ, 128
see also animals, as organ donors
Trull, Frankie, 142
Tudge, Colin, 168
Tulane Regional Primate Research
Center, 119

ulcers, 83
United Kingdom, 70, 137
United Nations Declaration of Human
Rights, 30
United Nations Food and Agriculture
Organization's Ethics Panel, 163
United States Department of
Agriculture (USDA), 36, 105, 111
and Animal Welfare Act, 36, 37, 42,
133–34
inadequate enforcement by, 101–102
University of California at San
Francisco, 105
USDA. See United States Department
of Agriculture
U.S. Patent and Trademark, 156